Praise for *The Dead Speak*

'*The Dead Speak* serves as a timely reminder of how meticulous a forensic expert must be — honest, tireless, and fiercely independent — to ensure justice is achieved.
And it is a captivating read, offering a wealth of ideas for legal counsel and expert witnesses working in criminal and civil litigation. In both simple investigations and the most serious cases, the outcome matters to those involved, and receiving the best forensic advice and guidance is crucial.'

Marie Dyhrberg KC

'Forget CSI — Tom Coyle takes you from Scotland Yard to the Canterbury quakes as part of a real-life journey into the world of forensic crime and disaster investigations.'

Michael Morrah, investigative journalist

'Fascinating, rigorous and underpinned by his expertise and humanity, Coyle's memoir offers a rare insight into the often-glamourised world of forensics.'

Fiona Sussman, author of *The Doctor's Wife*

The Dead Speak:

My Life in Forensics

Thomas Coyle MNZM

ALLEN & UNWIN
AOTEAROA NEW ZEALAND

First published in 2026

Allen & Unwin Aotearoa New Zealand
Level 2, 10 College Hill, Freemans Bay
Auckland 1011, New Zealand
+64 (9) 377 3800
auckland@allenandunwin.com
www.allenandunwin.co.nz

83 Alexander Street
Crows Nest NSW 2065, Australia
+61 (2) 8425 0100

A catalogue record for this book is available from the National Library of New Zealand.

ISBN 978 1 991142 38 2
Design by Cat Taylor
Set in Tiempos Text 10/18pt
Printed and bound in Australia by the Opus Group

10 9 8 7 6 5 4 3 2

FSC www.fsc.org MIX Paper | Supporting responsible forestry FSC® C001695

For Paul 'Webby' Webster and Joseph Stevenson,
who never had the chance to live out their dreams

Wherever he steps, whatever he touches, whatever he leaves, even unconsciously, will serve as a silent witness against him. Not only his fingerprints or his footprints, but his hair, the fibres from his clothes, the glass he breaks, the tool mark he leaves, the paint he scratches, the blood or semen he deposits or collects. All of these and more, bear mute witness against him. This is evidence that does not forget. It is not confused by the excitement of the moment. It is not absent because human witnesses are. It is factual evidence. Physical evidence cannot be wrong, it cannot perjure itself, it cannot be wholly absent. Only human failure to find it, study and understand it, can diminish its value.

Locard's Exchange Principle, Dr Edmond Locard (1877–1966), pioneering French criminologist

Contents

Introduction

As I look back, my sixteen years with the Metropolitan Police in London and almost fourteen years with the New Zealand Police seem to have passed in the blink of an eye. Yet in those 30 years I've accumulated a lifetime of impressions and memories, some of which I plan to share with you here.

During this time I attended and forensically examined over 20,000 crime scenes, and well over 200,000 exhibits in forensic laboratories. The crimes ranged from petty theft and car crime to burglary, armed robbery, assault, sexual violation and murder. I have witnessed first hand the terrible acts of violence people are capable of, whether premeditated or in moments of uncontrolled rage.

I have witnessed the dramatic evolution of forensic science over the years, affecting both the way we approach crime scenes and the analytical work carried out in laboratories. Gone are the days when ungloved investigators could wander through a murder scene, a cigarette in one hand and a sandwich in the other, leaving behind traces of themselves on critical evidence. These days, crime scene access is rigorously restricted, with only authorised personnel permitted to examine the area for evidence.

Over the past twenty years, crime scene investigation has been glamorised by TV shows such as *CSI: Miami*, *CSI: Vegas*, *CSI: Made Up* and *CSI :Stupid*. These fictional forensic examiners are portrayed as the heroes of the hour, with a vast knowledge of every field of scientific expertise. They enter the crime scene in their designer clothes and shiny shoes, wearing disposable gloves if you're lucky. They bend over a body, swishing their hair back to provide a sexy pose for the camera, and announce that they have just found a hair sample.

'What the fuck?' I am shouting at the television at the top of my voice. 'You have just shed ten of your own hairs all over the crime scene!'

Then there's the investigator who picks up a crucial piece of evidence and wraps it in a snotty tissue they produce from their grubby pocket.

Strangely, or should I say sadly, many people believe that these dramatised crime series portray reality.

Around twelve years ago I was presenting expert forensic evidence in the High Court at Auckland. After about an hour of hearing my evidence, the jury was released for morning tea. During this time the jury may discuss the case and, if they have a question about the expert evidence they have just heard, they can relay this to the judge. Well, they certainly did!

After the break I resumed my position in the witness box and the judge addressed me.

'Mr Coyle, I have a question from members of the jury regarding the evidence you are presenting today.'

'No problem, your honour,' I replied.

'Mr Coyle, you were at this crime scene for three days, during which time you preserved some of the evidence to examine back at your office. Then it took you another two weeks to identify the defendant who is present in court today.'

I knew where he was going. My heart sank.

'Some members of the jury,' the judge went on, 'watched an episode of *CSI: Crime Scene Investigation* last night, and in this programme the experts seemed to have examined the scene, compared the evidence and identified the suspect all within the hour. Can you please explain why it took you so long?'

I had to compose myself for a few seconds before replying, or my response might not have been very polite. During this time I felt some sympathy for the defendant, because his future depended on the ruling of these twelve persons who were supposed to be his peers.

I calmly addressed the eager jury members. During this unscripted presentation I shared the stark reality of what it's like to attend a crime scene. I walked them through the meticulous work involved in locating, developing and preserving trace evidence, as well as the role of the specialist scientists in laboratories who forensically analyse that evidence.

I further explained the complex processes put in place by

the police and forensic laboratories to ensure that the correct information is presented to the investigation team and prepared for the courts. 'It all takes time. It is nothing like the simplified, glamourised version you see on *CSI*,' I said.

The jury nodded collectively and wisely, with a few visibly blushing.

I wasn't one of these kids who dreamt from age eight of working in the world of forensic science. Far from it: I dropped out of college at the ripe old age of seventeen because I was bored and because most of my friends were out earning a wage and living the kind of life I wanted.

For the next year I tried my hand at many things: 'dogsbody' in a button factory, office admin, double-glazing salesperson . . . I really hated that one — wandering around the streets having doors slammed in my face.

I finally began work at Don Millers Bakery, a well-known establishment in the heart of Leicester City. There I found out I was damn good at baking — bread, savouries and cakes of all types. It was also during this part of my life that a violent crime resulted in the death of a close friend, which changed the course of my life. From baking pastries, I became a crime scene investigator.

Over the decades, technological advances have allowed forensic scientists to obtain information from evidence that was once incapable of telling us anything. When I first started, in the late 1980s, we had to swab an area of blood about the size of a 10-cent coin to determine a specific blood grouping. These days we only need a tiny blood sample, or even a simple skin swab, to obtain a DNA profile that can then be searched against a national database.

LCN (low copy number) or touch DNA profiling is becoming more sensitive every year through technology and research.

With advances in artificial intelligence (AI) it will soon be possible for computer software to work from a sample of blood and create a facial likeness of the donor. This technology has already been tested in four countries, creating up to 80 per cent likenesses of volunteers, and by the time you are reading this book it could well be that police services around the world are utilising this method.

I consider myself extremely lucky to have had a front-row seat on this rollercoaster ride. And I'm not done yet. Since my early retirement from the New Zealand Police I have pursued my love of forensic science as an independent forensic expert.

The word 'forensics' is derived from the Latin word *forensis*, which means 'of the marketplace or forum'. In Roman times, the forum was a public space where legal matters were discussed and decided. Thus, 'forensics' relates to the presentation of scientific evidence in an open court, and the application of scientific knowledge and methods to resolve legal problems. Forensic scientists work in a wide range of fields, including biology, chemistry, physics and earth sciences.

As well as working criminal cases, we are sometimes also called upon to attend mass casualty events to carry out disaster victim identification (DVI).

I refer to myself variously in this book as a forensic scientist, a crime scene examiner, a forensic practitioner and a fingerprint expert. All these descriptors fall under the same umbrella of ensuring justice is served through the scientific examination of evidence.

So, sit back, grab a cup of tea and a packet of chocolate biscuits, and maybe even a tissue or two, and we'll look back at some of the memorable moments of my career.

Oh, and fair warning that you may need a strong stomach . . .

Note: I have chosen not to include identifying details of the victims whose stories intersect with my work. Their privacy, and the dignity of their families, must remain protected.

Chapter 1

The Boxing Day Tsunami of 2004

On 26 December 2004 an earthquake with a magnitude of 9.2 struck off the west coast of the province of Aceh in Indonesia. It was the most powerful earthquake ever recorded in Asia, and the biggest earthquake of the twenty-first century. The quake produced tsunami waves up to 30 metres high, which devastated the coastlines of fourteen countries surrounding the Indian Ocean.

Whole communities were swept away and an estimated 275,000 people lost their lives. In some places around the coastline of Aceh, the sea receded so far that locals collected stranded fish and explored the exposed seabed before the waves crashed onto the mainland.

As the first fragments of news began to filter through, I remember being struck by images of utter devastation in places I had barely even heard of. Like so many others at the time, I was caught up in the holiday spirit — Christmas with family, sunshine, laughter, festive games, too much food and drink. But before long I would be in Phuket, Thailand, as a member of one of New Zealand's disaster victim identification teams.

By the next morning the holiday mood had dampened. Reports began to emerge of unimaginable destruction and a rapidly rising death toll, and it quickly became clear that international assistance would be essential — including the deployment of DVI teams. What I didn't yet realise was that New Zealanders were among the missing, and that behind the scenes the government and police were already racing to join an international response that eventually involved agencies and experts from over 30 countries.

In the daily life of a forensic expert, the crime scene is sacrosanct: time is taken to meticulously inspect and log each detail present in the hope of preserving the crucial, often microscopic piece of evidence that might prove a suspect, a motive, or a body identification. Sometimes, all three.

But in a disaster zone, all bets are off. The sheer numbers of dead can make the job of recovering the bodies seem an insurmountable task, let alone the forensic work of identification. You are working in extreme conditions, with hundreds, if not thousands, of families desperately waiting for news on their loved ones. The stakes couldn't be higher.

In the days that followed, every news channel and newspaper was consumed by images from the devastated regions. Scenes of disorder and human suffering filled screens and front pages: thousands of displaced families clutching the few belongings they had salvaged, queuing at makeshift relief stations for fresh water and basic food. Streets were lined with bodies, left out in the open by authorities already overwhelmed by the scale of the tragedy to deal with.

The initial New Zealand response was quickly organised, with the Defence Force deploying a 32-member Light Medical Team to work alongside the Australian Defence Force in Banda Aceh, the capital of Aceh province. Soon after, New Zealand's national DVI team, along with teams from around the world, began to converge on the region. Their massive operation would be based in Phuket, led by the Royal Thai Police. Other international DVI teams were deployed to Sri Lanka and Indonesia, but New Zealand was not involved in those.

I had joined the New Zealand Police only the year before, fresh from sixteen years in London's Metropolitan Police, and was still finding my feet. I was not part of the first New Zealand DVI team on the scene, but I was in one of the follow-up teams.

In the Thai provinces of Phang Nga, Krabi and Phuket, temples and other buildings were repurposed into temporary mortuaries. Due to the overwhelming number of bodies and concerns about disease from decomposition in the hot climate, army and government officials from some countries initially resorted to sending trucks full of bodies to mass burial sites.

The region was a hotspot for tourists, and the international teams initially focused on identifying these foreign nationals. The bodies were initially cooled with dry ice, until refrigerated containers arrived.

The multinational Thailand Tsunami Victim Identification Committee was formed on 12 January to coordinate the sharing of data from the different mortuaries, and to standardise DVI protocols and procedures based on Interpol guidelines. This helped establish chain-of-custody procedures for moving bodies.

I was delighted, yet apprehensive, when I was cleared to join Operation Phuket.

The night before I left, things were very emotional at home. My daughter Hannah was only twelve and visibly upset about my leaving to spend more than three weeks in a country she knew from news reports had been devastated. I tried to reassure her that I'd be safe, though I was struggling to convince even myself. My wife Allie and I had been together for over eighteen years and this was the first time I noticed she was nervous about a deployment. Yet she remained supportive, helping me convince Hannah that all would be well.

Early the next morning, Allie dropped me off at the airport for my flight to Wellington. There, we spent a full day in a classroom setting, receiving comprehensive preparation that included operational requirements, health concerns, a DVI refresher course, and lessons on Thai culture, customs and etiquette. The police commissioner turned up to wish us well, reminding us that we were representing not only the police but also the people of New Zealand.

The following morning we boarded Air New Zealand flight NZ407 for the initial leg of our journey to Singapore, where we would transfer to a flight bound for Phuket. The team on board included a forensic pathologist, mortuary assistant, forensic dentist, police photographer, inspector, superintendent and five other police officers with DVI experience. The atmosphere was unusually subdued; perhaps it was the early hour, or maybe everyone was feeling the same apprehension I was. Typically, when police personnel travel together, the air is filled with laughter and banter, but this was different. I think everyone was lost in their thoughts about what awaited us.

As the plane began its descent into Phuket, everyone was glued to the windows. The devastation we witnessed is a vision that will stay with me forever. Areas along the once bustling coastline were now desolate and empty, with only a few clusters of palm trees remaining. As we flew lower, the extent of the destruction became even more apparent: small groups of people were scattered across the land, desperately trying to recover anything the sea might have left behind.

After clearing Customs, we collected our luggage and were greeted by the outgoing DVI team leader, who looked utterly exhausted and seemed eager to return to New Zealand. He guided us to a minivan that would take us to our hotel. The drive was a sobering experience, as we saw close up the scale of the destruction that had befallen once-thriving coastal communities. We passed several concrete buildings that remained standing, their upper floors visibly marked by water damage. We learned that some of these structures had holes created by people desperately trying to escape the onslaught of water. Fishing boats were scattered inland, some perched atop buildings, carried there by the powerful waves.

Our hotel was the JW Marriott on Mai Khao beach, about 40 minutes from Phuket town centre. The hotel was located right by the sea but had undergone immediate repairs and then been commandeered by the Thai government to accommodate international DVI teams. It felt surreal to see this grand hotel, with its surrounding buildings and swimming pools, operating as if nothing had happened, while just outside its gates lay widespread death and devastation.

I was to share a room with Tim, the police photographer. Over the weeks that followed, we supported each other by talking daily about what we were doing, trying to remain grounded in these most challenging circumstances.

In a briefing room we were warmly welcomed by members of the team we were relieving. They had been in Thailand for three weeks and were returning to New Zealand the following afternoon. Their entire team performed a haka to welcome us and wish us luck with our deployment. The moment was charged with emotion; they were clearly physically drained, but many would have stayed longer if given the chance. We raised a toast and wished them a safe journey home.

The next morning, after breakfast, we were back in the briefing room to receive our assignments. I was assigned to the Thai Tsunami Victim Identification Information Management Centre

(TTVI-IMC) in Phuket town, to assist with victim identification. Though I was slightly disappointed not to be assigned to the mortuary, I understood the logistical challenges and said nothing. I boarded the minibus with five other team members for the 40-minute drive to Phuket. As we travelled south along the peninsula, the devastation we saw was indescribable. Entire villages had been flattened, with only a few buildings left standing. Locals were already trying to rebuild their lives, setting up makeshift homes and selling produce along the roadside.

We arrived at a centrally located building in bustling Phuket, provided by a telecommunications company to house the DVI operation. On the first floor we joined about 50 specialist personnel from around the globe. Fingerprint experts were working at makeshift AFIS (automated fingerprint identification system) screens. Forensic dentists were busy looking at dentists' X-rays. Another team was collating information from the mortuary to compare with overseas data on missing persons. At the end of the room was a small DNA section.

There are four phases to the victim identification process:

Phase one: The scene examination. Depending on the nature of the incident and its location, this may take several weeks. Some victims and property may never be recovered.

Phase two: During post-mortem, the human remains are examined for distinguishing characteristics: clothing, jewellery, fingerprints, dental information (odontology), DNA profile, scars, tattoos and even surgical implants that may be unique to the victim. This is known as PM (post-mortem) data.

Phase three: Known as the collection of ante-mortem (AM or pre-death) data, this involves interviews with relatives to collect information about the victim, including photos, medical and dental histories, and descriptions of clothing, jewellery and any other distinguishing characteristics. The victim's personal belongings, such as perfume or aftershave bottles, toothbrushes and hairbrushes are examined for fingerprints and DNA.

Phase four: Reconciliation. The post-mortem (PM) and ante-mortem (AM) data are collated, and experts within the relevant fields work to identify as many victims as possible. Only when there is a conclusive match between PM and AM data can the body be released to the family.

The focus of our team at the IMC was phase four: reconciling ante-mortem and post-mortem data to establish connections. PM data, collected from the victim, was documented on pink Interpol DVI forms, while AM data was recorded on yellow forms.

We entered this information into a specialist computer system developed by Plass Data. When the system suggested a potential match from fingerprints, DNA or dental records, we manually verified the data to confirm or exclude the identity. If it looked like a match, the section leader re-examined the findings before they were presented to a reconciliation board for final approval. At that point a death certificate was issued, and the body was released to the national authorities of the victim's country.

I was the team leader for the fingerprint identification station, with the responsibility of ensuring that all identifications were thoroughly peer-reviewed and verified. I was also honoured to be chosen as the forensic fingerprint expert on the reconciliation board.

On the first day, I sat down at my desk and observed the bustling room filled with experts from around the world. Everyone was united in a single mission: to identify victims of the disaster and send them home to their families, providing them with a sense of closure. I introduced myself to the other fingerprint experts, who had travelled from the UK, Australia, Israel, Sweden, Finland and Holland, and was relieved that they all spoke English — some better than me.

On one wall, a large whiteboard displayed the names of victims who had been identified but who we knew had deceased family members still awaiting confirmation. Where possible, family groups were kept together to be sent home at the same time. I vividly recall a family from Sweden — a mother, father and son — who had been identified but were waiting for us to locate and identify another son, who might have been separated from them during the tsunami. There was a collective urgency to find this final family member so they could all be returned to Sweden together.

As I was familiarising myself with the procedures and protocols, a bell suddenly rang out in the office, prompting everyone to stand and cheer. I was told that the bell signalled a positive identification, meaning another repatriation. The bell would ring up to fifteen times a day, and it never failed to bring a smile to my face.

At lunchtime we headed down to the ground floor and enjoyed a hearty Thai meal, beautifully prepared by locals. It always tasted as good as it looked.

Before I knew it, my first shift was over and, along with the rest of the New Zealand team, I boarded the minibus back to the hotel. There, we headed to the briefing room to meet up with colleagues from the mortuary team, and swapped stories over a cold beer. The superintendent updated us on the day's achievements, including the number of bodies officially identified, and praised us for our efforts in such challenging conditions.

Back in my room, I showered, changed into civilian clothes and headed down to the restaurant to join some others for dinner. Seeing fresh local lobster on the menu, caught that day, I couldn't resist ordering it with a side salad. As I tucked into my meal, I noticed some locals watching me. Eventually a German colleague approached with a knowing smile.

'You must be new here,' he said in a thick German accent.

'Yes, I arrived yesterday,' I replied.

He leaned in and shared a secret. 'None of the locals are eating seafood right now. They're selling it cheaply to hotels for the workers because there are likely to be many bodies still in the sea. These lobsters may be feeding on human remains on the seabed.'

I stared at my half-eaten lobster, unsure whether to laugh

or cry. From then on, I avoided seafood, opting mostly for vegetarian meals.

The next day I returned to the IMC to continue verifying fingerprint identifications made by officers searching the AFIS system. In the afternoon I was asked to provide the final expert verification of several identifications to the reconciliation board, which met in the makeshift coroner's court on the building's second floor. The board was presided over by a high-ranking Thai police official, assisted by two associates. On one side of the room sat the IMC experts representing fingerprints, dentistry and DNA, while on the other side were officials from various Thai forensic science centres, there to approve our findings.

Being part of this board, representing over 30 countries, was an incredible honour for me. In my statement I provided the victim's name, date of birth and country of origin, and reported the verified match between AM and PM fingerprint data. The other experts provided similar verifications within their fields of expertise. The Thai official seated opposite confirmed our findings, the paperwork was stamped, and the body was authorised for release.

In the minibus back to the hotel that day, each of us sat quietly gazing out the window, lost in our thoughts. To break the silence, one of the officers asked the driver to play one of his personal CDs. As 'Take Me Home, Country Roads' by John Denver began to play, someone started singing along, and within moments we were all belting out the lyrics together. From that day forward, this song became a staple of our rides back to the hotel, often played on repeat. We knew every word by heart and it became our anthem, sometimes bringing smiles, and at other times a tear or two.

After a week at the IMC I was eager to see if I could transfer to the mortuary team to assist with the examination of the deceased. The superintendent helped coordinate my request, and the following day I swapped teams. Before heading to the mortuary on that first day I was briefed by the forensic pathologist and dentist, who updated me on procedures and the condition of the bodies.

The mortuary we were heading to was in the village of Takua Pa, near Khao Lak beach. The Buddhist temple Wat Yan Yao had been transformed into a makeshift mortuary and served as the main hub for international DVI teams from Australia, Germany, UK, Belgium, New Zealand, US, Singapore, China, Scandinavia, France and the Netherlands and other countries.

On the journey I admit I felt a bit nervous — not because of the body examinations, which I had done many times before, but because of the overwhelming number of them. As we approached the temple I noticed its distinctive entrance: a large pillar either side supported a three-tiered pyramidal roof. Each elaborate tier was adorned with gold paint.

Just inside the entrance was a small building where Thai officials were fielding public enquiries about missing loved ones. Behind the public counter were large viewing boards filled with photographs of bodies, displayed in the hope that family members might recognise someone. It was pretty obvious why so few were in fact identified this way — the violence of the disaster had caused gross disfigurements.

We came to an entrance marked 'DVI Personnel Only' and guarded by Thai army officers. Inside the complex, rows of refrigerated metal cargo containers each held around 50 bodies awaiting examination. At any given time, the facility had about 500 bodies on site, with an additional 600-odd stored securely down the road. In that moment, a wave of sadness washed over me, accompanied by the sobering realisation of how fragile life is — how, in an instant, the sheer force of nature can so easily wipe us out. Makeshift trolleys with handwritten 'taxi' signs were being used by Thai army personnel to transport bodies to and from the mortuary.

In the centre of the dusty yard stood a large marquee, with white plastic chairs scattered around various tables. Behind it was the mortuary, curiously bearing a sign that read 'Opera House'. Beyond the mortuary stood the temple itself, its beauty a stark contrast to the surrounding scene of death.

The air was heavy with the odour of decomposition. Scented joss sticks had been strategically placed around the complex to hide the smell from the public on the busy street outside, creating a blend of sweet-sour that was quite overwhelming in the 30–32°C heat.

While most people outside wore shorts and T-shirts, we

donned full personal protective equipment (PPE) to protect ourselves from exposure to the decaying bodies. The heat as we worked was intense, causing constant sweating and underlining the need for us to stay hydrated.

Working inside the mortuary were experts from many countries. The facility was divided into four sections, each designed to gather PM data, and the bodies were moved through the mortuary in a specific sequence: photography, fingerprints, pathology and odontology.

The mortuary process began with the team leader requesting a body from one of the storage containers. Two Thai army soldiers retrieved the next available body bag and transported it in a 'taxi', positioning it on a table. The body was assigned pink DVI forms, each marked with a unique reference number.

Next, two DVI-trained police officers carefully opened the body bag and a photographer captured the body in its untouched state. The officers then removed any clothing from the body, recording details such as manufacturer marks, size and design name. Any unique markings were recorded — especially any engraving inside wedding rings. The officers similarly documented and photographed any tattoos. The clothes and jewellery were taken outside to a special cleaning bay, sprayed with fresh water to remove any grime, and bagged and labelled with the same reference number. Finally, the pink PM forms were cross-checked by the team leader.

The body was then moved to the fingerprint section, where experts employed various techniques to record the ridge detail of the finger and palm prints. This process was thorough, ensuring that every ridge was captured accurately. In cases where fingers or hands were missing, this was noted on the pink DVI form. For added precision and quality assurance, the recorded fingerprints were cross-checked to ensure there were no errors or omissions.

After fingerprinting, the body was transferred to the pathology section for a comprehensive examination, external and internal, by a forensic pathologist. The pathologist recorded details such as height, weight and any body modifications, and noted any missing limbs. Additionally, they examined the body for surgical scars, including those from plastic surgery, to build a complete profile. Internally, the pathologist sought to determine the cause of death and checked for surgical implants. During this stage, DNA samples were collected from various bones.

Finally, the body was moved to the forensic dentistry section, where experts recorded the dental configuration, including details of any fillings, caps and false teeth, as well as analysing the alignment of each tooth. In some cases the forensic dentist would remove the lower jaw to get a better view of the teeth.

With all the detailed examinations complete, the team leader collected all the pink paperwork related to that body for a final review. The documents were then sent to the IMC for the information to be entered into the Plass Data computer system. The 'taxi' was then called to return the wrapped body to the container it came from.

I was assigned to the fingerprint workstation, where it quickly became apparent that capturing fingerprints would be challenging because of decomposition. We would need to use special methods. The two main types of decomposition we encountered were putrefaction and mummification, each requiring a different technique.

During putrefaction, the body is rapidly decaying, emitting foul odours, and becoming wet and mushy. The epidermal layer of the skin detaches from the dermal layer, so when the body bags were opened, the skin was often found floating in the goo and ooze released from the body. We had to reach into the odorous goo to retrieve the skin from the hands and feet, and clean it with soapy water. We would then place the skin of the deceased's fingers onto our own hand, like a glove, and record the fine ridge detail using black powder and white sticky labels, or black ink on a specialised fingerprint form. This process is known as de-gloving.

During mummification, the body is exposed to the sun's heat and loses its fluids, causing the skin to become leathery and hard. This makes it impossible to record ridge detail from the hands, so we used the 'boiling hand' technique. We placed the hand in a wok of boiling water for about 30 seconds, causing the pores to open and allowing water to enter and stretch the skin. Then we dried the hand with a towel, whereupon the pores would close, and we could then use standard fingerprinting techniques to record the ridge detail.

Interestingly, after using this method on several bodies, my colleagues and I began to feel hungry, despite the overwhelming smell from the cadavers. We had been reusing the same water in the wok, and bits of skin were accumulating, causing the water to smell like chicken soup. From that point, we made sure we changed the water regularly.

During breaks we would leave the mortuary and make our way to the seating area under the marquee to rest, rehydrate and take in some lungfuls of fresh air. The first day at the mortuary was exhausting but it was also extremely rewarding, knowing that the information we obtained would be used to identify numerous bodies and allow their families closure. Most of the time we had no idea which country the body initially originated from, but we could tell many were tourists, judging from their clothing and tattoos.

The first day seemed to end as quickly as it began, and honestly, I wanted to stay longer, but our exposure to the bodies was strictly limited. On the drive back to the hotel we passed a boat that had become a landmark for Thai residents. Police Boat 813, *Buretpadungkit*, had been anchored about 1 nautical mile off the coast of Khao Lak at the time of the earthquake. The crew were assigned to protect Poom Jensen, grandson of the King of Thailand, who was jet-skiing in the bay. The tsunami claimed Jensen's life, and the first wave picked up the boat and carried it over 2 kilometres inland to Bang Niang. Moving it posed a logistical challenge due to its massive weight, so the government decided to leave it where it lay, as a memorial to the disaster.

Back at the hotel, the first thing I did was to call Allie and Hannah — to hear their voices, make sure they were okay, and let them know I was safe. This connection to home was always comforting and served as a reminder of how precious life was. We were reminded daily of how quickly it could be taken away.

The next few days flew by as we established a smooth process for fingerprinting the bodies. It became clear that most of the deceased had not died by drowning in the tsunami. Rather, they had suffered fatal injuries from debris swirling in the fast-flowing waters, which severed arteries, leading to significant blood loss. Numerous victims also had badly broken bones and severed limbs from impacts with vehicles and buildings.

One morning I was working in the mortuary when a Thai official approached and asked if someone could assist in examining fingerprint data to confirm the identities of two victims believed to be government officials. I volunteered and, with the mortuary manager's permission, headed to an official government building. There, two Thai fingerprint experts were struggling to match prints from a body with AM data. I examined the ridge detail from a thumbprint recorded from the body and compared it with a thumbprint taken from an item found in the individual's house.

The main problem seemed to be the limited information available for comparison. I requested a brighter light and a more powerful magnifier to closely examine the fine minutiae along the ridges, as well as the creases and enlarged pores. After 40 minutes of close examination I informed the Thai experts that in my opinion the print obtained from the house was identical to that from the deceased person and I was happy to sign the official paperwork for their records. The second comparison was far less tricky and I confirmed the identity within five minutes, to the relief of the Thai officials.

The next morning I was asked to assist with several more tricky cases where decomposition was advanced. A Thai official escorted me to another mortuary nearby to examine three bodies that had suffered prolonged exposure in water. Severe open wounds exposed bones, and the faces were unrecognisable — bloated and discoloured. One body had no eyes, and part of the nose was missing.

The epidermal skin was loose but not completely detached so I was able to find the hands relatively quickly. Skin fell away from several of the fingers, so I used the de-gloving technique to record the detail. The rest of the fingers still had skin attached, and I was able to record these by using black powder. I got finger and palm prints from all three victims and provided these to the grateful officials.

I spent numerous days at the DVI mortuary, successfully extracting clear ridge detail from many bodies. To broaden my expertise, I also spent time at other forensic stations, immersing myself in various different aspects of forensic mortuary procedures.

While our work was demanding, we were given some downtime to relax and explore Phuket and the surrounding area. It was truly humbling to witness the resilience of the Thai locals. Despite the devastation they had faced, they remained positive and grateful for our assistance. New homes were already being built along the coast, and people were making concerted efforts to return to normalcy in the midst of enormous personal losses.

While exploring the devastated areas we noticed a number of fishing trawlers washed inland. Two in particular stood out: they had been lifted by the waves and dumped on the roofs of buildings, left balancing precariously when the water receded. In one village every single structure had been destroyed and swept away by the waves — except for one. In the centre of this barren landscape stood a small church with a red roof, seemingly untouched by the devastation. It was as if the waves had parted around it. Most of us who beheld this sight found ourselves looking up to the heavens, offering a silent prayer.

On several occasions we ventured into the heart of Phuket to enjoy the nightlife at local bars, with a particular favourite being the Crazy Horse. This venue welcomed police personnel, providing a space where we could relax without attracting the attention we drew on the streets. One memorable night the commander from the London Metropolitan Police, who was the DVI lead for all the participating countries, joined about 40 other police officers from around the world. At the end of the bar was a bell, and tradition dictated that anyone who rang the bell planned to shout drinks for everyone. The commander was in high spirits that night and rang the bell at least ten times, keeping the shots flowing freely.

By the evening's end we were taking turns dancing on the bar with locals. Some Thai police officers patrolling nearby joined us for a couple of drinks before resuming their duties. Needless to say, we all ended up a bit the worse for wear, and luckily we Kiwis had the next day off. Shame about the others: I can't imagine having to face the mortuary's odours with a hangover.

Another time we visited the memorial wall in Mai Khao, Phuket. Stretching for about 70 metres, the wall displayed the flags of all the countries that suffered losses in the tsunami. Some sections were adorned with pictures of the missing, placed by families still waiting for news. We all stood there, observing a moment of silence to honour those who had lost their lives.

We also took the opportunity to visit a local market renowned for its array of 'designer' items, albeit counterfeit, including DVDs, watches, trainers, clothing and handbags. The craftsmanship was so impressive that it was really hard to distinguish some of these items from the genuine article. Despite being police, we couldn't resist the temptation to buy a few items, rationalising it as a way to help the locals rebuild their lives. I ended up buying a 'Tag' watch, which I still have today, along with a few T-shirts and DVDs of movies that were just being released in cinemas. I was curious about how the traders managed to acquire these items, but they told us with straight faces: 'They are real, not fake.' They even added: 'If you find they are fake when you return home, you can come back for a refund', which brought a smile to my face.

During my final days of duty in Thailand, I returned to the Information Management Centre to continue working in the forensic fingerprint section. Our team was successful in identifying many foreign tourists, and several times I presented evidence to the reconciliation board. One afternoon, while I was verifying an officer's work, two high-ranking Thai officials came to the office and asked the IMC manager to halt all activities. They called me over and presented me with a Thai police memorial, in recognition of my contribution in assisting their officers in the challenging task of identifying bodies through ridge detail analysis. It was a special moment, for me and for the New Zealand Police, who already held a prominent reputation in the international DVI community.

My last day at the IMC was a whirlwind of emotions. On the one hand, I was eager to get back to my family, but on the other, I felt a twinge of sadness at leaving unfinished business. I would have gladly stayed to continue the vital work we were doing.

Just before lunch, a wave of excitement rippled through the office when a team member's jubilant scream confirmed that we had just identified the young boy from Sweden who was part of the family of four. It was a profoundly moving moment, and tears of relief and joy were shared, along with hugs, while applause resonated throughout the room. Knowing that the family would be reunited and travel home together was a poignant reminder of the significance of our work.

Back at the hotel we were greeted by the new DVI team from New Zealand, who were set to take over our duties for the next three weeks. They looked sheepish and nervous, reminding me of how I had felt when we first arrived. We reassured them about the meaningful work they were about to undertake, and warned them to steer clear of the seafood! That evening we shared our experiences and insights at a formal dinner, highlighting how the individual efforts of each team member were interdependent, with one role seamlessly supporting another to achieve our common goals.

During our flight back to Auckland the superintendent stood up to address us once more, thanking us for our work. His tone shifted as he continued. 'I realise that many of you visited a certain well-known market selling counterfeit items.' We exchanged nervous glances, feeling the weight of his words. The super continued. 'I must remind each and every one of you that I do not condone the purchase of these items, and being caught with them could lead to serious consequences.' At this point we were all anxious, knowing that most of us had acquired at least one counterfeit item, and some were carrying quite a few. Then, with a mischievous wink, he added: 'Anyway, now that I've mentioned this, I have two Tag watches and three DVDs the same if anyone is interested in a swap.'

We were greeted at Auckland Airport with a powerful and moving haka in the VIP arrivals area. This emotional welcome was followed by a warm greeting from the police commissioner, expressing gratitude on behalf of both the police and the country for our service in Thailand. We were told to head straight home, with a mandatory minimum stand-down period of seven days before resuming official duties. This would prove a much-needed time to rest and recover. Then we were reunited with our families in the arrivals hall. The warm smiles radiating from both Allie and Hannah's faces as they saw me emerge is a memory I will cherish forever.

Before resuming official duties, it was also mandatory for every active DVI member to attend a debriefing session with a psychologist. The intention was to ensure that we were not experiencing flashbacks from the intense and distressing scenes encountered during our assignment, and to confirm that we were mentally prepared to return to work. This support system was invaluable in maintaining our well-being and readiness for future challenges. Once cleared, I returned to work, ready to face my next demanding adventure.

The work in Thailand continued for many months, and by the end of 2005 the DVI process there had identified a total of 2894 tourists and Thai citizens recovered from all over the country. Many more were buried without being identified, underscoring the challenges faced in such tragic circumstances.

Chapter 2
Growing Up on a Council Estate

I have vivid memories of the highs and lows of my childhood in Leicester. I recall many happy times in which my friends and I messed around Braunstone Park. We'd climb trees, build dens from discarded bits and pieces, and just do what kids do — or did before cellphones. Explore.

My father left us when I was a toddler and my older sister Tracy was four, and we moved to a council house in a large estate on Erdyngton Road. After a year or so Mum met a Geordie from the heart of Sunderland in the north of England, who ended up becoming my stepdad. In time there were two further children, Amanda and Neil, and the four of us ended up being a close-knit group of siblings.

I can recall some good times as a family, but after a few drinks my stepdad could become violent, especially towards Mum. The worst of these incidents was the evening of Christmas Eve 1979. We were all excited to open the presents under the Christmas tree, and had been trying to figure out what each one contained from the shape of the packaging.

That night, though, my stepdad was really drunk, and when Mum said something he didn't like, he lost it big time. He shouted and punched and kicked her with such ferocity that the sound appeared to echo around the hallway. We tried to stop him but were met by flailing fists, so just ended up huddled together on the staircase, crying and screaming with each blow that rained down upon our mum.

At the end of the beating he seemed to realise what he'd done and bolted out the front door.

Mum was in hospital for a week.

As was the way at the time, Mum had kept the truth of the violence she suffered hidden from other family members. They all knew there were problems but she never wanted to talk about it. This time, however, it was impossible to keep it a secret. Her seven brothers made sure a message got to her husband never to return . . . and he didn't. I haven't seen him since.

Life was tough growing up on a council estate. I was a skinny streak and most of my friends were bigger than me, including the girls. To avoid being bullied, I used humour as my shield. It worked most of the time.

Despite this, my years at secondary school were some of the best of my life. The building was over a century old, crumbling in parts, and never saw a single refurbishment while I was there — but I loved it. Those worn corridors had a certain magic.

I was drawn to the stage and surprised myself by landing parts in school productions. My biggest moment came playing the lead in *Oliver!*, an end-of-year show the school actually splashed out on. Four sold-out nights, a spot on the news, and hundreds of T-shirts with my face on them. I felt like a local celebrity.

At age fifteen I had three close friends: Paul 'Webby' Webster, Glenn Laffar and Richard Kilbourne. Each had his own unique personality and personal baggage. Paul was a carefree type, always socialising and enjoying life. Glenn was family-focused, and already head over heels for a girl named Patricia Taylor (they eventually got married and are still together). Then there was Richard, who seemed content with the idea of staying in Leicester forever.

As for me, I always felt Leicester was not meant to be my permanent home. I had a burning ambition deep inside, a feeling that one day I would leave it all behind — my family and my friends — and set out on some adventure that was waiting for me. Like most young people around me, I had run-ins with the police. Back then we respected the 'boys in blue'; in some cases we even feared them. I remember on one occasion I was messing around on the roof of our school with a friend, and somebody saw us and called the police. They turned up just as we were climbing down the drainpipe and arrested us for burglary. We got a fright, but pretty soon the police decided we weren't worth all the paperwork, so they let us off with a stern warning.

Another time Glenn rode past my house on a 49cc Yamaha FS1 — also known as a Yami Fizz — and called out, 'Hey up, Tom, want to go for a ride?' So of course I jumped on the back. We sped off up the main road — in my mind we were doing about 70 miles per hour but it was probably closer to 40. Before I knew it, blue lights were flashing behind us. Glenn gunned the throttle all the way down and the engine screamed to its maximum revs, trying to outrun them, and then he turned to me, shouting at the top of his lungs, 'We need to jump off soon and run — the bike's stolen!'

In that moment I panicked, gripping his side and yelling, 'Slow down, you're going to kill us!' We reached a part of the road that led to a field, and Glenn stopped the bike.

'Run as fast as you can!' he said.

I didn't need any convincing. I sprinted as fast as my legs could carry me, glancing back after about 30 seconds to see him being handcuffed and put in the back of the police car. I didn't know what to do. Should I hand myself in or just keep quiet? I chose the latter, as we were in our final year of high school and I was earmarked to go to sixth-form college to obtain my A levels.

Glenn was charged with a few offences, but he never gave away that I was the passenger. A true friend. Still, I admit I was absolutely terrified for days afterwards, expecting a rap on the door at any moment, but it never came.

Every July, a fairground would set up at one end of Braunstone

Park, staying for two weeks before moving to New Parks for another fortnight. The rivalry between these two estates had been ongoing for as long as I could remember, and those four weeks when the fair was in town seemed like the perfect time to settle which had the toughest reputation.

To set the scene: Braunstone Park and New Parks were each set among thousands of council houses, separated by Hinckley Road and a railway line. A bridge crossing between the two estates acted as a neutral zone. When the fair came to town, the bridge became the gathering place for youths to test their strength in various ways. Most of the time it was just kids throwing things at one another across the bridge, but now and then, two lads would call each other to the centre for a one-on-one scrap.

The police, in their usual way, tended to let things unfold. They knew it was an annual occurrence, and usually no one was seriously harmed.

However, one year things escalated after one of the girls from Braunstone was assaulted at the fairground by some lads from New Parks. The following day a large group of older boys from Braunstone showed up on the bridge, intent on retaliation. They were armed with Molotov cocktails and other weapons, turning the situation into something far more intense. It quickly resembled a scene from Belfast in the 1970s and a number of people were injured.

The police arrived with riot shields, trying to restore order, while a helicopter hovered overhead to help ground patrols track the movements of individuals involved. Around fifteen people were arrested, and the bridge was closed for two weeks.

By the time I reached the ripe old age of sixteen I had a forged driver's licence to get me into nightclubs. I had to bulk myself out, so whenever I ventured into the city centre for a night out I wore two T-shirts, a thick shirt and a thick jumper under a more casual top. It did the job, but shit, was I hot inside those nightclubs.

One night I struck up a conversation with a girl, and at the end of the evening we exchanged home phone numbers (no cellphones of course back then). Afterwards, my four friends and I found ourselves at a bus shelter, even though we knew there were no buses at that hour. We were happily recounting the night's adventures when a group of eight to ten young men approached us, demanding to know which of us had been chatting up one of their girlfriends. Outnumbered and significantly smaller than these guys, we fell silent, which only fuelled their anger. Suddenly one of them lunged forward, grabbed me by the throat and pinned me against the glass. 'It was you, you bastard!' he shouted, and started to punch me.

In that moment of chaos my loyal friends ran away, with two of the attackers chasing after them. Realising I was alone and in serious trouble, I felt a wave of fear wash over me. 'Fucking have him!' one of the guys shouted, and for the next several minutes they took turns punching and kicking me as I struggled to defend myself. After sustaining around twenty blows to the head, I managed to curl up on the ground in a ball. For what felt like hours they continued to kick me until eventually they grew bored. When the two lads who had pursued my friends returned, they all walked away, seemingly satisfied.

My mates finally came back to find me on the ground covered in blood. My saving grace at this point was that I was drunk, so the injuries didn't feel too bad. In fact I got up, with blood streaming down from my nose and a cut above my eye, and wanted to go after them for round two. My friends managed to dissuade me and took me to hospital instead.

Lying in a hospital bed, I became aware of intense pain radiating from my face and chest. Panic set in when I ran my fingers across my face and discovered that a partial facemask had been plastered over my nose and cheeks. A nurse explained that I had sustained significant injuries to my head and body, and needed surgery to reconstruct my nose and restore my ability to breathe easily.

I felt a wave of anxiety. Would I end up looking like the Elephant Man? He came from Leicester . . . Like any young man in my position, my main concern was whether my injuries would affect my dating prospects.

I vividly remember my mum coming to see me, tears welling in her eyes. I hadn't noticed her walk past all the beds in the ward and eventually turn and run out, distressed. One of the nurses led her back to my bedside. With the severe bruising and the plaster mask she hadn't recognised me.

I spent five days in the hospital while the doctors monitored my condition and ensured that the bruising was gradually subsiding. It was another three weeks before they removed the cast from my face, and three weeks more before the bruising had completely faded away.

Six weeks later, restored to rights, I attended a party with Glenn, and towards the end of the night a fight erupted among a group of guys, escalating into a full-blown brawl involving most of the guests. When I saw one guy hitting Glenn, I instinctively jumped in to defend him. Suddenly I felt a sharp pain as someone landed a punch squarely on my nose. I immediately sensed that my nose was broken again, and blood began to pour down my face. Over a two-year span I broke my nose three times, and even now I struggle to breathe properly on one side.

After finishing high school I was pleasantly surprised to learn that I had passed all my General Certificate of Secondary Education (GCSE) exams in eight subjects, and also achieved five O levels. I considered this a significant accomplishment, considering I hadn't studied much. I was accepted into a sixth-form college to pursue my A levels, and since I was unsure about a career, I decided to seize the opportunity and continue my education.

Chapter 3
A Baker, a Sailor, a Fingerprint Taker

I formed a deep dislike for sixth-form college. I felt disconnected from the other students and struggled to make meaningful friendships. To make matters worse, I had somehow ended up choosing the worst combination of subjects: geography with pure and applied mathematics. I wasn't even good at maths! I still don't know how I got sidetracked into those subjects, but it felt like a huge mistake.

My friends from the estate were working, enjoying their newfound freedom, going out, and spending their hard-earned money. I, on the other hand, was still dependent on my mum and only managed to work a few hours at weekends at Superdrug, a store that paid minimum wage.

At age seventeen I felt as though my life was going nowhere, and as if I was missing out on important experiences. As my first year of college ended, my attendance began to dwindle and my grades took a nosedive. My motivation waned, and the prospect of obtaining better qualifications started to feel increasingly irrelevant. After failing a couple of mock exams I decided to quit. To say that my mum was disappointed would be an understatement. She had always envisaged me being the first in our family to achieve academic success.

I moved from job to job until Richard, a baker's assistant, helped me secure an interview at Don Millers Bakery where he worked, and where I was offered the position of assistant baker. The catch was the hours of work: I was required to work very early mornings from Monday to Wednesday, and night shifts on Thursday and Friday. Being an early riser, I found this schedule manageable. I loved the work, and quickly began to excel in my role.

One of our most popular items was the doughnuts. When the doughnuts came out of the fryer, they were rolled in sugar while still hot, as the oil helped the sugar adhere. However, there were times when the doughnuts were left to cool for too long. I vividly remember witnessing Richard licking cold doughnuts before rolling them in sugar to make it stick. I have never eaten a doughnut since.

The owner recognised my potential, and after just one month asked whether I would be interested in attending college once a week to become a qualified baker. The company would cover the cost. I eagerly accepted, and for the first time I felt a sense of optimism about my future.

I thrived at Don Millers, and my creativity began to flourish. I started experimenting with new pastries, many of which I had learned about at catering college. I still confidently maintain that I was the one who invented the savoury delight of bacon and grated cheese inside filo pastry. These creations became immensely popular and we sold thousands.

After nearly a year I was happy in the thought that baking would be my career for many years to come. The owner trusted me to manage the shop if he or the manager were away, and I enjoyed that added responsibility. Life was good.

But everything changed on the evening of Friday, 7 November 1986.

I arrived at work around 10 p.m. for my night shift and immediately got to work preparing ingredients. I placed everything in an industrial-sized mixer to create the dough for our various breads and rolls. Since we were located in the city centre, surrounded by bars and nightclubs, it was quite common for my friends to drop by of an evening when they were feeling peckish. They would pop in for a free doughnut or the occasional out-of-date roll. One of my regular visitors was my good friend Paul Webster, who was always eager to snag a treat.

Around 11.30 that night there was a commotion on the street outside, with people screaming and shouting. We all stepped outside to investigate. Someone told us there had been a fight near the clocktower, an iconic monument in central Leicester, and some people had been seriously injured. I could see blue flashing lights illuminating the buildings and heard the wailing of police sirens approaching from all directions. Since we were just around the corner, I decided to go and see for myself, and what I encountered was a grim scene.

Police were working to contain the situation, and I saw officers attending to two injured people lying on the ground. Ambulances soon arrived and paramedics swiftly took over tending to the victims. The atmosphere was tense and chaotic.

Suddenly I saw that one of the young men on the ground was my mate Webby. I was frozen in place, unsure of what to do. All I could do was stand there, staring at the strangers around me who were desperately trying to save his life. But their efforts were in vain — Webby died from a single stab wound to the heart.

The scene was surreal and heartbreaking, leaving me grappling with disbelief and an overwhelming sense of loss. I later learned that there had not in fact been a fight. A seventeen-year-old youth who was either drunk or high on drugs had run down the street brandishing a large knife. He charged into a group of people, including Webby, and, without any provocation, stabbed him in the chest. The youth then ran further down the road and attacked an unarmed police officer who was patrolling the area, stabbing him in the back. The inspector recovered from his injuries but he never returned to the streets.

The community was devastated by the news of Webby's death. I had known him for most of my life, and my intense grief transformed into anger and frustration. I was furious that Webby had been taken from us through such a senseless act of violence. I felt powerless and frustrated because there was nothing I could do to help bring the perpetrator to justice.

After months of soul-searching and countless nights spent

crying into my pillow, I finally came to the realisation that I needed to make a change. I understood that I needed to direct my anger towards something constructive.

I decided to leave Leicester and explore two potential career paths: either joining the Royal Navy or becoming a police officer. On discovering that there was a lengthy waiting list for police training, and that they were mostly seeking candidates with more life experience, I chose to enlist in the navy.

I passed the basic naval entrance exams with flying colours and received a call-back. They were so impressed with my results that they were recommending me for the Naval Officers Training Programme. I was stunned; it felt like a dream come true. All I had to do was pass the medical examination, which I naturally assumed, being young and fit, would be a breeze. I honestly believed securing my place was a foregone conclusion.

On the day of the medical I took a bus to the examination building in the town centre. It was an old Victorian structure that bore signs of age. As I entered through the set of oak doors with frosted glass panels, a nurse greeted me and led me into a room that seemed to have been frozen in time. The furniture looked to be pre-war, and the air was thick with the smell of decades of cigarette smoke.

The doctor, who I took to be in his sixties, instructed me to strip down to my underpants and step on the scales. 'You're a bit skinny and underweight,' he remarked in a voice that had a peculiar drone.

'I'm trying to gain weight by going to the gym,' I said quickly.

He mumbled something in response and then gestured towards a pair of headphones, I assumed to check my hearing. 'Listen for any tones in your left or right ear and press the button if you hear them,' he instructed.

Finally, it was time for me to complete the basic physical test. I was told to jump up on a pole positioned between two walls and hang from it for 30 seconds, then perform twenty pull-ups. As I completed my fourth pull-up, I caught my nose on the pole and heard that unmistakable crack. Before I knew it, blood was rushing down my chin and onto the floor.

However, I was determined not to quit. I pushed through the remaining sixteen pull-ups and was then instructed to do 30 press-ups. I don't think the doctor even noticed the blood smeared across my face and the floor, so I quickly wiped my face and continued. By the end of the exercise I looked as though I had just gone a few rounds with Mike Tyson. I felt exhausted.

At this point the doctor noticed the blood and my deteriorating condition. Realising I was on the verge of passing out, he ordered me to sit down and called a nurse. She managed to stop the bleeding and tried to soothe me, mentioning that I might need to go to the hospital to have my nose checked, as it could potentially be broken.

I felt tears welling up inside. After about 30 minutes the doctor called me back into his office. While my overall health was excellent, he said, I needed to gain 20–25 pounds before he would sign me off for the Naval Officers Training Programme. I was given six months to bulk up to the required weight.

I threw myself into training, hitting the gym as often as my body would allow. I started taking every weight-gaining supplement I could afford. The regime paid off: I began to put on weight and build muscle mass. Just as I was starting to feel confident about finally making it into the navy and escaping Leicester for some exciting adventures around the world, life threw me another curveball. I met the love of my life, Allie.

Allie's brother Kev was dating my sister Amanda, and they were practically inseparable. The first time I met Allie was at a New Year's Eve party at the local workingmen's club. I was there with my fiancée, and Allie was attending with her boyfriend of two years. We found ourselves sitting opposite each other, and I couldn't take my eyes off her. From that moment, I knew I had to get to know her better, so I asked if she would like to go out for a meal as friends.

As was often the case in Braunstone, a large brawl broke out at the New Year's Eve party, involving some of my family and friends. Like a fool, I jumped right into the fray to protect them, which did not impress Allie at all. Her reaction made me realise that I needed to exercise more care and consideration if I wanted her to stick around.

Nevertheless, a couple of weeks later we went out for a meal and it was immediately clear there was a spark. We had to keep our relationship a secret, which added a thrilling sense of forbidden romance. After a few discreet meetings we decided it was time to come clean to our partners and families. My fiancée was very emotional but surprisingly understanding. Allie's boyfriend did not take the news at all well, pestering her for several weeks to reconcile. Our families were also less than pleased, particularly Amanda and Kev. But Allie and I were flourishing, and we both knew we were meant to be together.

Then out of the blue I received a call from the navy offering me a spot in the training programme, conditional on my having gained the required weight. I was torn. While I craved a new direction in life, the thought of leaving Allie for extended periods to go to sea was daunting.

My thoughts drifted back to the police. Since Webby's murder I had felt a strong desire to help victims of crime, particularly those who were unable to advocate for themselves. I grappled with feelings of inadequacy regarding the physical requirements for frontline police duties, but the prospect of sitting in an office handling reports all day did not appeal to me either.

One evening, while watching a television programme about crime scene investigations, featuring an investigator in a white suit meticulously searching for evidence, I realised that this was precisely what I wanted to do. I was also acutely aware that I lacked the necessary qualifications for such a role, and that opportunities for this work within the police were limited.

I started scanning national newspapers for relevant job vacancies. As luck would have it, I came across an ad for a trainee fingerprint officer at New Scotland Yard in London. It wasn't quite the crime scene examiner role I had initially envisioned, but it would be a good start. Without hesitation, I contacted the recruitment office and requested an application form. I filled it out with enthusiasm, sending it back the very same day.

Two weeks later my mum received a call from the police recruitment office. I had been selected for a job interview in London. Mum was asked to advise me to be prepared for a long and challenging day. I was overcome with a mix of excitement and anxiety, pondering what kinds of tests I might face during the interview.

I set off for London, stepping into the big unknown. Navigating London alone is daunting, with hundreds of people all rushing to their next destination, mostly avoiding eye contact. The Underground was a new experience for me. I hadn't realised just how deep below ground some of the stations were, and I could see why they had been used as air-raid shelters during the war.

I finally arrived at the police recruitment centre in the heart of Westminster. Upon entering, I was met by a crowd of other candidates, all vying for the same position. I later learned that over 400 people had applied for just ten openings. After some more form-filling, I sat down to wait. As I sat there, I tried not to glance at the other candidates; I knew that if I did, I might feel overwhelmed and tempted to walk out. Instead, I focused on calming my nerves, reminding myself how much this opportunity meant to me.

I was finally ushered into a small room with about twenty other candidates and asked to sit at one of the vintage-style desks. Our first test was a basic assessment of our skills in maths and English, followed by a fingerprint matching exercise. After two hours of focused effort, we were all directed into another room to undergo eyesight and colour-blindness tests. Individual interviews with senior officers from New Scotland Yard rounded off the day. This was the moment I had been dreading.

In front of me, slightly elevated from the floor, sat five middle-aged men who looked stern and authoritative. Without introducing themselves, they began asking me questions about my life and my reasons for wanting the position. As the interrogation progressed, I felt increasingly out of place and uncomfortable; my shoulders slumped, and my gaze began to drop towards the floor.

After about fifteen minutes of what felt like an intense grilling, I was on the verge of getting up and leaving when one of the interviewers said, 'Mr Coyle, can you please describe a pencil?' I looked up, wondering if it was some sort of joke. However, after a moment of reflection I took a deep breath and replied, 'It has a graphite core encased in wood, and you must sharpen one end to create a point. You can then write with that end until it becomes blunt, at which point you use a sharpener to restore the point so you can continue writing. You repeat this process until the pencil is too small to use anymore, at which point you discard it and get a new one.'

I looked each interviewer in the eye in turn, feeling a sense of calm wash over me. 'Thank you, Mr Coyle. You may go,' one of the men said.

I stood up and left the room, confused and relieved, unsure what had just happened.

The journey back to Leicester felt long and lonely as I reflected on the day, convinced that I had messed up. I found myself engaged in a silent debate with my subconscious, replaying some of the stupid responses I had given during the interview. I couldn't shake the feeling that I had made a complete fool of myself.

I resigned myself to the idea that I would continue with my mundane life in Leicester.

About two weeks later a letter arrived from the police. I almost didn't bother opening it, fully expecting a generic 'thanks but no thanks'. Eventually I gathered the courage to rip open the envelope, and to my absolute astonishment, I was being offered a position at New Scotland Yard.

I could not contain my excitement: I started running around the house like a madman, screaming and shouting until my mum came in to see what all the commotion was about. 'Mum, Mum, I got in!' I exclaimed, tears streaming down my cheeks.

'Got into what? Hopefully not trouble!' she said, looking concerned.

'I got into New Scotland Yard to train as a fingerprint officer!' I was overcome with joy. This was a dream come true, and the thrill of the moment made all the challenges worthwhile.

The following weeks were quite surreal. I had to keep rereading the letter to make sure I wasn't dreaming. The reality finally sank in when I received follow-up correspondence from the police, requesting references and notifying me that they were conducting security background checks.

During this time I was spending more and more time with Allie. I didn't want to risk going out with the lads, getting drunk, and potentially landing in trouble that could jeopardise my chance to go to London. Not to mention my relationship with Allie. Nope, I thought to myself, you need to keep a low profile. Stay out of trouble, and be a good boy.

A week before I was set to start my new position, an incident occurred that could have thrown everything. One night, around 10.30 p.m., I was walking home from Allie's house, taking my usual route. It was a twenty-minute walk. As I turned onto the upper end of Erdyngton Road, two police cars suddenly pulled up beside me. Before I could fully comprehend what was happening, I found myself being roughly pushed into the back of one of the patrol cars.

From the front seat an officer asked, 'What are you doing out here all alone at this time of night?'

'I'm just coming back from my girlfriend's house,' I replied.

'We've received a report about a person matching your description, wanted for a very serious offence. We're taking you to the station for questioning.' With that, the door slammed shut and we were on our way to Charles Street Police Station.

My heart was racing: this was the last thing I needed. The timing could not have been worse.

I was led into an interview room, where a detective from the Criminal Investigation Department (CID) sat down across from me, with a uniformed officer standing by the door. The detective spoke in a calm voice. 'Okay, son, what's your name and date of birth?'

'Why, what have I done?' I nervously replied.

'Name and date of birth first, then I'll tell you why we've detained you.'

I reluctantly gave him the information, and he quickly left the room, presumably to check my name in their database to see whether I had had any prior trouble with the law.

After five minutes he returned, seemingly disappointed. 'Looks like you have no previous convictions, so why were you walking down Erdyngton Road at that time of the night on your own?'

By this point I was extremely scared, so I explained in detail, pointing out that I lived about 30 houses down the same road.

The detective explained that the night before, at the same time, a person matching my description had raped a young woman at knifepoint in a house nearby. Before leaving the premises, the assailant had told his victim he would return the following night to finish what he had started.

A cold chill ran down my spine as I absorbed this information, and I began to shake. 'It's not me, I promise you. I know that girl — just ask her,' I pleaded.

'Don't worry, we'll be speaking to her again in the next couple of days,' the detective reassured me. After asking a few more questions they finally took me home, escorting me inside to verify my address. They pulled my mum aside to tell her about the night's events. Once they left, I broke down in tears. But mum's first question was 'Was it you?'

'I can't believe you're asking me that!' I shouted back in anger. I rushed to my bedroom and slammed the door behind me, seeking solace in the darkness of my room.

The following afternoon, as I wrapped up my shift at Don Millers, a police car was waiting for me outside. They drove me back to the police station to continue the interview. I had a rented videotape with me, which I had watched a few nights earlier and planned to return that day. As soon as I entered the interview room, it was the first thing they looked at. The film was *A Nightmare on Elm Street*, featuring the iconic image of Freddy Krueger on the cover, with his infamous glove adorned with knives protruding from the fingers. The detective, sounding almost eager, asked, 'Do you like this kind of thing? Mutilation and knives and harming other people?'

Immediately nervous, I replied, 'It's just a horror movie. I watched it with some friends.'

For the detectives, my watching this incredibly popular movie was something they could latch onto. The atmosphere in the room was tense, and it hit me just how much they knew about me — everything from my previous jobs, schools, family and, strangely enough, my new position at New Scotland Yard, which I had mentioned in passing during the previous night's interview. After two hours they finally told me I could go — but I could not leave Leicester.

Right, as if I had a passport and the means to flee and start a new life in another country . . .

Over the next 24 hours I experienced a whirlwind of emotions. I was angry at being accused of something I didn't do, but also fearful about the impact this could have on my future. It soon became clear to me that New Scotland Yard had been made aware of the allegations against me in Leicester.

Out of the blue, the detective in charge of the case arrived at my house, asking to speak to both my mum and me. This was it: they were about to arrest me. The anxiety was overwhelming: I saw my wonderful new world come crashing down around me.

But that was not what happened. The detective began by thanking me for my cooperation during the interviews. He apologised for the distress I had experienced, and explained that they had spoken with the victim, who had confirmed that she knew me and that I was not the perpetrator.

I slumped back onto the sofa in relief. I felt I could finally breathe again. The detective then handed me a letter addressed to the Metropolitan Police, which exonerated me of any wrongdoing and thanked me for my cooperation during their investigation. With that, he left.

I forwarded the letter to the police recruitment office. They responded quickly, confirming my trainee position, beginning in three days.

The day finally arrived: it was June 1988 and I was leaving Leicester to pursue a new career in a city that was a complete mystery to me, aside from what I had read about in books. Allie, naturally, was emotional about the departure, but found some comfort in knowing I would return most weekends to see her. As I boarded the coach, I waved goodbye before heading off into the unknown.

I made my way to the police accommodation, known as The Regina, and settled into my modest room. It was as basic as could be, furnished with just a wardrobe, a chair, a table and a bed. The facility included a shared common area with a TV, as well as communal kitchens and bathrooms. This would be my home for at least the next six months.

The following morning I headed to Monck Street in the heart of Westminster for our induction. There I met the nine other recruits who would be embarking on this journey with me. Among them was Matt, a tall, good-looking guy with an effortless charisma that drew attention wherever he went. We instantly clicked, sharing stories about our backgrounds and where we were from.

The course instructor asked us to introduce ourselves one by one to the group. When it was my turn I stood up confidently and said, 'Hi, my name is Tom Coyle, I'm from Leicester, and I'm staying at The Vagina.'

The room erupted with laughter — even the instructor couldn't suppress a chuckle. It took me a moment to process what I had just said, and then it hit me. In one awkward but unforgettable moment I had branded myself as the funny northerner. Well, if I was going to make an impression, that was certainly one way to do it.

Chapter 4

From Fingerprints to Maggots

It took five years to train as an authorised fingerprint officer.

The first module would take eight weeks, and for the first few days we spent time settling into the classroom, getting to know each other, and handling official paperwork, including signing the Official Secrets Act. In that moment, of course, I pictured myself as 007 — minus the chiselled good looks, the sports car and the beautiful women.

On the second day we visited New Scotland Yard and I was filled with eager anticipation. I can honestly say I was not disappointed.

People sometimes ask me about the origin of the name New Scotland Yard, as many assume, logically enough, that it comes from Scotland. However, the name has its roots in London. It dates from the nineteenth century and the old building in Whitehall Place that used to house the Metropolitan Police headquarters. The main entrance faced a street called Great

Scotland Yard in Westminster. Over time, the term Scotland Yard became synonymous with the police headquarters. In 1890, when the police moved to a new building on the Victoria Embankment, it was referred to as New Scotland Yard. Then in 1967 the headquarters relocated once again, this time to a newly constructed building on Broadway in Victoria. The iconic name, which by then had worldwide recognition, remained.

That building loomed before me, an imposing eighteen-storey structure with an eight-storey annex to one side, adjacent to Victoria Street. At the front, a massive three-sided display slowly rotated, showcasing the name: New Scotland Yard.

Inside, my eyes were immediately drawn to the vast reception desk, centrally positioned in the expansive waiting area. Behind the desk, security and reception staff kept a vigilant watch, scrutinising the security badges tucked in visitors' plastic pouches or black police leather wallets. Since our security ID had not yet been issued, we trainees gathered in a corner of the room waiting for our instructor to sign us in. At either end of the reception desk were the only two entry points to the building, each manned by additional security personnel.

The interior of the building was a labyrinth, each floor branching off into secure rooms that housed some of the most secretive and powerful departments, including anti-terrorism, murder, fraud, child abuse, anti-corruption and the gang squad. The air was thick with smoke. In the 1980s, smoking was not only permitted, but sometimes even encouraged to help calm the nerves.

Staff members, for the most part, were impeccably dressed: the men in shirts, suits and ties; the women in blouses and skirts. The only floors where staff entry was restricted were the seventeenth and eighteenth, which housed top-tier personnel, including the commissioner of police. You knew you were in trouble if you had to report to one of those floors.

The fingerprint section spanned the sixth, seventh and parts of the eighth floor in the adjacent annex building. When I started, in 1988, the section had around 200 staff engaged in analysing prints developed and preserved from crime scenes, and comparing them to those of people previously arrested. There were no computers to store the vast number of prints taken from suspects or the associated paperwork. It all had to be completed manually.

Staff were split into several teams, each with specific tasks.

During our eight weeks in the classroom we learned about skin structure, ridge formation, and fingerprint classification and identification. There was a lot more to the study of fingerprints, or dactyloscopy, than I had realised. We also learned a lot of fun facts about fingerprints and their use in crime-solving.

For example, the oldest known images of hands showing ridge detail are prehistoric drawings discovered on a cliff in Nova Scotia, Canada, dating from around 200 BC.

The first murder case solved using fingerprints dates back to 1892 in Argentina. A 27-year-old woman named Francisca Rojas was discovered in her home with severe throat injuries. In the bedroom were the bodies of her two children: six-year-old son Ponciano and his four-year-old sister Feliza, both with their throats slit. Rojas claimed that her neighbour, Pedro Ramón Velázquez, had attacked her, then killed her children.

Velázquez was arrested, and it was reported that he endured a week of torture in an attempt to extract a confession, including being tied down in the bedroom with the bodies of the two deceased children. Throughout this ordeal, he consistently maintained his innocence.

The authorities contacted Inspector Eduardo Alvarez, who had been trained in fingerprint analysis. Alvarez examined the crime scene and discovered a bloodied fingerprint on the inside of the bedroom door. He removed the door and set up an examination area back at the local police station. He then obtained fingerprints from Francisca Rojas and compared them to the bloodied print from the door. Noticing that the shape and pattern closely resembled that of Rojas's right thumb, he used a microscope for a more detailed comparison. Eventually, he confirmed the bloody fingerprint as hers.

During the subsequent interview, Rojas broke down and confessed to the murder of her children. It was revealed that she had fallen in love with someone new, but there was a significant obstacle to their relationship: he did not want her children. Tragically, Francisca Rojas chose to kill her children in the hope of starting a new life.

Ultimately, all she achieved was a life sentence.

We found out that a person's fingerprints are formed before birth, and remain unchanged throughout their life, barring injuries. If such an injury occurs, the resulting scar will be permanent and can serve as a unique identifying feature. Interestingly, while identical twins share the same DNA, they have different fingerprints. This is because fingerprints are not genetic; instead, they develop based on various factors to do with the mother during the early months of pregnancy. Factors such as how the mother sat, how she slept and what she ate influence the way the foetus moves in the womb. As the hands and feet push outwards they create unique patterns in the skin, leading to the formation of fingerprints.

Every person's fingerprints are unique. In fact, even with advances in technology, fingerprints remain the only universally accepted form of identification worldwide. This lasting uniqueness is why fingerprints remain important in forensic science and personal identification.

The three main fingerprint pattern types are whorl, loop and arch, and each has innumerable variations. Have a look and you'll see that the lines (ridges) on your fingers, palms and feet don't run continuously but form patterns, especially at the ends of your fingers.

At the end of each training day we were left to our own devices. Our accommodation was pretty dismal and depressing, so most evenings we'd head out to one or two of the many bars across London. This gave us a chance to unwind and also to get to know one another.

For the last two weeks of the first course, we had to learn how to classify fingerprints using a formula called the Henry Classification System. The Henry system took the basic shapes of arches, loops and whorls, and developed a complex mathematical classification system that produced 1024 possible fingerprint types. Sub-classifications followed.

The formula was developed in 1896 by Sir Edward Henry, assisted by Hem Chandra Bose and Qazi Azizul Haque, as a way of classifying fingerprint shapes. Sir Henry was an administrator in India and introduced the use of fingerprints there to sign legal documents. He was later appointed assistant commissioner at New Scotland Yard and head of the CID.

This was, without a doubt, the most challenging part of the course, but it turned out that I was pretty good at it, managing to achieve a perfect score in the final exam.

Each part of the course had an exam at the end, and we had to achieve a minimum of 80 per cent in each one, so the pressure was on, but this didn't stop us leaving our revision to the last minute, cramming in a few last-minute sessions, often a bit drunk. If you failed three exams you were out — kicked off the course and out of the police. We knew it had happened in the past, but fortunately, at least in the initial stages, we all seemed to be getting through okay.

After the initial eight-week course we were seconded for six months to the coding section on the sixth floor. The idea was that this would give our eyes and minds a chance to become accustomed to looking at fingerprints. Well, that was the spiel.

In reality, it was an exercise in monotony and boredom.

We later found out that the coding section was notorious within the bureau. The mind-numbing work was perfect for new recruits — they would throw us in the deep end and see how long it took before we cracked under the monotony. Each day we'd receive hundreds of inked fingerprints from individuals arrested across London. Like an assembly line of robots, we'd quietly sift through the prints, analysing the lines and patterns to form a readable classification. Once classified, the prints were sent to the relevant fingerprint teams before being stored in the massive collection on the seventh floor.

The long, tedious days were broken up by the constant banter that bounced between colleagues — and by the tea breaks. Every morning at 10 a.m. a tea trolley would roll out of the lift and the tea lady would ring a handbell, summoning us all from our rooms like the Pied Piper calling children from their villages. Before long a queue would form, with everyone eager to buy an iced bun or scone to accompany their strong tea or weak coffee, each served from a large silver urn. It became a part of our daily routine within the secretive walls of New Scotland Yard, and we all looked forward to it.

A few years later, when the staff canteen on the third floor was upgraded, there was no more tea trolley. To say we were annoyed would be an understatement. The commissioner insisted it was the way forward, but we all missed the tea lady with her stale baked goods and lukewarm beverages, which had brought so much simple joy to our dull lives.

Finally the six-month secondment ended and we were transferred to fingerprint search teams. We were going to work on real cases, trying to identify real criminals based on the fingerprints they left behind at crime scenes. The office I joined consisted of a dozen people, across a wide range of ages. I was the youngest, and some were well into their retirement years. Each of us had our own personality and sense of humour, but we all had one thing in common: we loved a drink, which was an all-too-familiar bond between staff at New Scotland Yard.

Our team's role was to evaluate the fingerprints submitted by scenes of crime officers (SOCOs). During this time SOCOs were all police officers and it was their job to examine crime scenes to gather any and all information that may constitute evidence to link a suspect to the crime. It was classed as a 'dirty' position and usually filled by officers who were fed up with frontline duties and happy to work alone.

They examined items using a squirrel-hair fingerprint brush and aluminium powder to dust for prints. If prints were developed, the SOCOs would preserve them by applying a special tape over the print and then placing this on a piece of clear plastic. The preserved prints would be submitted to the fingerprint section for comparison and identification.

Our first step within the fingerprint team was to evaluate the quality of the prints to determine whether there was enough information within the ridge detail to identify a person. If a print passed the quality threshold, we would ascertain which finger it likely came from (thumb, fore, middle, ring or little), identify the pattern type and then classify the limited fingerprint characteristics present within the fingerprint ridge to make it searchable.

Next, we would compare the print against the elimination prints taken by the SOCOs from people who lived at the address or location where the crime was committed. Once those people were ruled out, any remaining prints would be checked against those on file for known local criminals. Each section maintained its own mini-collection of fingerprints, and it was surprising how many identifications we made using this method.

If no matches showed up, that's when the real hard work began. We would head up to the seventh floor, where the complete fingerprint collection was housed. When I saw it for the first time I was stunned by the sheer size of the collection. How could anyone possibly find a match among this endless sea of ink? I asked myself.

The collection occupied half the floor, stored in sixteen purpose-built cabinets holding a total of about 5 million fingerprint forms — 50 million individual finger and thumbprints. Not surprisingly, the seventh floor was a secure area with restricted access.

The prints were organised according to their Henry classification, and our job was to try to match crime scene prints to one of those inked sets in the collection. It was a daunting task that demanded patience and persistence. It was like a treasure hunt. Officers could spend hours manually searching through the prints, hoping to find a match. If you found one, the sense of achievement was enormous because it was you and you alone who had identified that suspect. It was quite a high.

The fingerprint collection served another, less official purpose: it became a quiet spot where staff members would gather to gossip, particularly about colleagues. And on those occasions when we returned from a long lunch a little worse for wear, it was the perfect place to have fun with colleagues in the same state.

I remember one Friday afternoon, after a particularly extended lunch at a bar, I ended up in the collection with four others. One of them dared another to start mixing up bundles of fingerprint forms, taking one stack and combining it with another, and then another. It wasn't exactly a brilliant or responsible idea, but at the time it seemed like a fun thing to do. All I can say is that if you were a criminal and your prints were stored in one of those bundles, that was your lucky day.

As the first few months passed, I became increasingly proficient at identifying crime scene prints. I developed a knack for coding the prints in the correct order, which made the manual search process much more efficient. I was successfully identifying individuals linked to all types of crimes, and I was genuinely enjoying the role. However, in the back of my mind I longed to be out in the field, examining crime scenes first hand. Despite that, I had resigned myself to spending several more years focused on fingerprints.

The first year flew by and there were rumours of huge changes ahead for all those working within forensic science, internally and externally. The technology was changing rapidly and there was also growing concern about cross-contamination between serious crime scenes. The three personnel who attended major crime scenes were the SOCO, a fingerprint expert and a forensic scientist from Lambeth Laboratory. The commissioner wanted to streamline this so that only one person would attend, and was looking at introducing a new role incorporating all three disciplines.

The long-awaited announcement finally took place, introducing a new role: identification officer. SOCOs and fingerprint staff were given the option to either remain in their current positions, in which they would no longer attend serious crime scenes (unless requested), or transition to this new role. The forensic scientists were not eligible as they were not police personnel. The new position involved additional training in forensic science.

It was an easy decision for me. Having worked in the fingerprint section for sixteen months, with many years of training ahead before I would qualify as an expert, I opted instead to expand my skills: to process crime scenes and collect all types of forensic evidence, not just fingerprints.

I knew the training would be intense, but I was excited for

the challenge. Surprisingly, most of the SOCOs chose to stay in their current roles, and even more unexpectedly, many of the fingerprint staff opted to remain within the bureau full-time. But for me, this was the moment I had been dreaming of, and I wasn't going to let it sail by.

My training from now on would combine the fingerprint modules with instruction in an extensive range of forensic topics, including forensic detection and recovery, the interpretation of hairs and fibres, footwear impressions, tool marks, broken glass, blood spatter, arson investigation and cadaver examination. I would need to complete a course every four to six months for the next three years before I would be allowed to go out into the field.

Just after the announcement was made, my fingerprint training course visited the local mortuary to observe a post-mortem and learn about the work of forensic pathologists. We assembled outside Westminster Mortuary, waiting for the pathologist's assistant to come and escort us inside. The assistant briefed us, saying that if any of us felt faint or unwell we should raise our hand and they would escort us out. Alternatively, as she put it, 'just run'.

Westminster Mortuary, built during Victorian times, showed its age in every corner. Soot-staining on the brickwork, a remnant of London's coal-burning past, was evident both inside and out. Two large wooden oak doors led into a cold, damp waiting area furnished with old wooden pews. It was the first time I had encountered the smell of death: decaying bodies mixed with the scent of cleaning fluids. How did pathology staff ever get used to this smell? With their clothing and skin absorbing it as they went about their day, they likely took the stench home with them at the end of each shift.

We were ushered through two sets of swing doors, feeling like lambs to the slaughter, and finally we entered the main mortuary room. The cadaver in question, covered by a white sheet, lay on a stainless-steel gurney attached to one of the many wash stations around the room. The stained tile walls and the trolley of dissecting equipment completed the impression of a scene from an old Sherlock Holmes film. The smell of the body was instant and overwhelming and hit me like a ton of bricks.

The pathologist entered the room, cigarette in hand, casually puffing away as though he were taking a leisurely stroll in the park. He stubbed out the cigarette in a half-full ashtray on the countertop. He was in his fifties, tall and lanky, with silver hair slicked back so perfectly it almost seemed artificial. Dressed in a white plastic butcher-style apron, he approached us and announced that the body we would be examining was a 'floater'. I'd been in the police long enough to know that this meant the body had been found in water, most likely the River Thames.

'This one's going to be a stinker,' he said with a grin. 'If this is your first time, rub this gel under your nose. It'll help.'

He handed around a small container of gel, and we took turns dabbing some under our noses. The sharp scent of mint flooded my senses, rushing up my nostrils and down the back of my throat, clearing my airways instantly. However, it did little to mask the overwhelming smell that was beginning to settle in my chest.

As I stood there, I felt a strange mixture of curiosity and disgust. The pathologist's calm demeanour contrasted sharply with the gruesome scene before us. The body of a mature male in his sixties lay on the gurney, bloated from days spent submerged in water. Flies had taken no time at all to find the body, drawn to the stench of decay, and had set up home and laid their offspring in all easily accessible areas. Those maggots now oozed from the eye sockets and ears, voracious in their appetite for flesh.

The pathologist hadn't even started and I knew the smell was going to get *much* worse. He casually examined the body, noting a few visible injuries that might shed light on the cause of death. Then his technician helped him heave the body over, sending a cascade of maggots tumbling to the floor. It was a surreal sight, the writhing maggots searching for shelter in the chaos. After inspecting the man's back, they flipped him over again, releasing yet another wave of maggots. Right in front of me was a vivid but grim reminder of nature's cycle of life and death.

The atmosphere within our group shifted as the pathologist made his first incision, a scalpel gliding beneath the right collarbone with unsettling precision. With a single fluid motion he carved a Y-shaped entry into the body, pulling back the skin to expose a yellow layer of fat that clung to the inside surface of the skin and the ribcage. The assistant swiftly retrieved a large cartilage blade, slicing through the ribcage as though it were soft butter, expertly removing a portion and setting it aside.

It was at this point that things started to get interesting. The pathologist was a very animated guy who liked to gesticulate while explaining what was happening and describing each organ's significance. Like a character out of *The Muppets*, he set about boisterously removing the organs one by one. I remember blood hitting my face and clothes as bodily organs were swung about, and it was at about this point that I felt queasy and had to turn away for several seconds to compose myself.

Then it was time for the lower intestines to be removed, and shit — excuse the pun — did they smell. It was a disgusting mixture of decaying flesh, rotten blood and aged faeces.

But the worst was still to come.

With the organs now collected in a large silver bowl, the pathologist moved to the head, making an incision from ear to ear around the back of the head. He then pulled the skin up the back of the skull and down over the forehead, resting the wadge of skin and hair on the deceased's nose and exposing the skull in all its glory. The assistant handed the pathologist a glistening instrument connected to an electrical device to cut through the bone. I can still hear that saw — the gruesome sound of grinding metal and splintering bone. Particles of bone were sent flying and the smell of burning filled the air.

The cap of the skull never comes away cleanly, so a hammer and chisel were brought in and soon enough, with a large crack and pop, it was off. The brain was duly scooped out for the pathologist to examine.

The whole PM procedure had taken only 40 minutes (though

it felt like a *lot* longer). It now fell to the technician to put all the organs into a single white plastic bag and place it neatly inside the stomach area. The ribcage was placed back into position and the skin was folded back over, ready to be sewn back together. After some brain samples were removed for further research, the brain was placed back in the skull, and everything pushed and pulled back into place to reveal the deceased person's face again.

I made my way back to my new rented flat, which I was sharing with Allie. She had bravely decided to leave her job in Leicester to join me in London, a testament to our young love. That evening, upon entering the flat, I was met with the unmistakeable aroma of liver and onions, one of my favourite meals. Normally I would have been ecstatic.

In front of me lay a generous portion of sliced pig's liver, the scent creeping down my throat and mixing with the lingering stench from the mortuary. I tried to eat it, to force the food past my gag reflex, but then, without warning, the smell of the deceased surged back and I couldn't do it. I rushed to the bathroom, where I instantly vomited in the toilet. I was now surrounded by three heady smells in combination: the cadaver, the liver and the vomit.

It was quite a day.

Chapter 5
Work Hard, Play Hard

One of the most challenging aspects in my early training was identifying deceased individuals who were found without identification or were too decomposed to be recognisable.

It was routine during the late 1980s to go to the mortuary to obtain the fingerprints of the deceased. The pathologist would remove the person's hands at the wrist and place them in a jar filled with formaldehyde to stop them decomposing. It was our job to take these to the Lambeth Laboratory for analysis. It was the strangest feeling walking through the streets with a jar containing somebody's hands. You wanted to make quite sure you didn't drop them on the way . . .

From these hands the fingerprint expert had a multitude of techniques for extracting the best prints. These ranged from basic powdering or ink methods right through to specialist moulding and photography of the fine ridge detail. It took a bit of getting used to, handling body parts in this manner, but I was young and followed established protocols without question. Afterwards we returned the hands to the mortuary, where they would either be reattached to the body or placed with the other organs inside the stomach area.

A pivotal moment changed this practice, triggered by a maritime disaster. On 20 August 1989 two vessels, the *Bowbelle* and the *Marchioness*, collided on the Thames. The *Bowbelle*, a dredger, struck the *Marchioness*, a pleasure boat, twice at the stern, causing the latter to capsize. The *Marchioness* was carrying 131 people, and tragically 51 lost their lives that day.

A major incident response was initiated to identify the deceased and return them to their families. In an attempt to expedite the process, as the bodies accumulated at the mortuary, the pathologist at the time made the decision to remove the hands of about 25 victims for fingerprint analysis. Unfortunately this led to a cascade of problems when miscommunication and the absence of proper records meant the hands could not be matched to the corresponding bodies. Ultimately, most victims were identified through visual recognition and personal belongings, with only four identified through fingerprints.

The situation became even more heartbreaking when some families were given the wrong bodies, and one family received their loved one without hands attached. This fiasco was a significant blow to the reputation of the police and prompted an urgent call for procedural changes in the handling of large-scale incidents.

Within twelve months of the *Marchioness* disaster, the

protocols had undergone significant change and the removal of hands was prohibited. Instead, we had to time our mortuary visits to occur before or during the PM, to ensure that the bodies were not in the refrigeration unit, and take prints directly from the bodies. (Obtaining accurate prints from a refrigerated body is virtually impossible.)

On one occasion I found myself at the mortuary alone, waiting patiently for the pathologist to complete their examination. I struck up a conversation with the pathologist's assistant, who was busy collecting and bagging organs. It was like watching someone on a grotesque shopping trip.

The needlework skills of the mortuary assistants were seriously impressive. With an oversized needle and thread they expertly pulled the skin edges together, creating a neat seam. While it wasn't on par with the delicate work of a plastic surgeon, it was sufficient to mask the fact that just twenty minutes earlier, every bodily organ had been laid out on the examination table for inspection.

That part of the procedure complete, I received the nod to begin fingerprinting. I had a case containing all the essential tools: a torch, various powders, brushes, ink and paper. I also had a post-mortem strip holder and a selection of finger straighteners. The strip holder was a simple device designed to hold a strip of paper in place against the finger while I recorded the print.

The finger straighteners, also known as post-mortem print spoons, on the other hand, resembled something out of a medieval torture chamber. We used them to straighten fingers that were still in rigor mortis or tightly clenched. It was a tricky procedure and it wasn't uncommon for the practitioner to apply too much pressure, leading to the unsettling sound of a finger cracking under the strain. I vividly recall the first time this happened to me: the sudden noise sent a shiver down my spine and I dropped the straightener on the floor in surprise.

Fortunately, on this particular day the body I was examining was in good condition, requiring no medieval devices. I was recording the fingerprints when the assistant re-entered the room, wheeling in another body. This new arrival was placed in one of the examination bays to my right. After securing the wheels of the gurney, the assistant left the room. The mortuary was dimly lit, with only one overhead light illuminating the body I was working on. The other body was obscured in the shadows.

A few minutes into my examination, I was startled by a strange sound emanating from the other body, which was covered by a white sheet. The noise stopped, and I shrugged it off and continued with my task. A short time later the noise began again, becoming increasingly pronounced. I looked across and suddenly the body shifted ever so slightly. I watched in horror as the head lifted up — just a little, but enough for me to freeze in terror. Then, with an alarming gushing sound, the head fell back onto the gurney. I nearly wet myself.

That was when I heard the pathologist's assistant, now back in the room, laughing so hard he nearly fell to his knees. What the hell was happening?

Once the assistant had calmed down, he explained the phenomenon I had just witnessed. Apparently bodies in the morgue often 'talk' to one another, due to the build-up of gases produced during decomposition. These gases escape through various orifices. In this case the deceased's bowels were likely blocked, so the trapped gases were forced up the oesophagus, but his tongue had slipped down the back of his throat, blocking the airway. The gases had accumulated and the pressure built up until it was strong enough to push the tongue forward, causing the head to rise briefly before falling back.

Since that day I have often heard bodies 'communicating' with one another, but I'll never forget that first time . . .

On another occasion I was again alone in the mortuary to examine a cadaver. My task was to record the finger and palm prints in an effort to identify the individual, who had died in suspicious circumstances in a local park a few hours prior. With no wallet or identification found on the body, determining their identity was crucial for notifying the next of kin.

I had successfully obtained the prints from the right hand and was examining the left palm when the hand suddenly clenched, as if the deceased were trying to grasp my fingers. I froze and dropped my equipment to the floor. My eyes darted up to the face of the cadaver, and in that surreal moment I found myself wondering whether the person had somehow come back to life. It sounds ridiculous, but what other explanation was there?

Once I regained my composure and realised that the movement was simply a result of muscle contraction due to the onset of rigor mortis, I held the hand down and then continued with my examination.

Lurking in the background at New Scotland Yard was a pervasive old boys' network, especially among middle and upper management. The phrase 'If you don't like it, you know what to do' echoed through the halls, and they meant it. There was no support system in place for staff who regularly faced the trauma of crime scenes and the horrors of the mortuary — no counsellors, no psychologists, no team leaders. Many of my peers bottled up their emotions, and even today several are grappling with PTSD symptoms due to the lack of support during those challenging times.

I think this is why in those days most personnel at Scotland Yard played as hard as they worked. Drinking was a normal part of the job and a socially acceptable way to let off steam. Don't get me wrong — it wasn't as if the building was full of people who were too drunk to solve crimes, but outside of work many would let their hair down. In the basement of Scotland Yard there was a bar called The Tank. This establishment served as a sanctuary for police employees, allowing us to discuss the day's events over a pint without the risk of being overheard by the public. Although the bar comfortably accommodated 30–40 people, it was not uncommon for over a hundred of us to cram inside on Friday lunchtimes, eager to take advantage of the low-priced drinks.

Being a young chap, I never turned down an invitation to join my colleagues at The Tank. Those Friday lunches often blurred into the afternoon, especially if our boss was part of the group. When we finally emerged from the bar, somewhat the worse for wear, we would make our way back to the office, collapse into our chairs and pretend to be productive. Sometimes the boss would reveal their hidden stash of whisky in the desk drawer and the merriments would continue.

At the end of the day, or when the whisky ran dry, we would all head across the road to a public bar named The Feathers, another police haunt. Here, we would spend the evening laughing, singing and generally having a bloody good time. Those days the bar staff continued to serve you until you called it quits or your funds ran dry — or until you collapsed in a heap on the dirty floor.

As I reflect on those late Friday nights, I can't help but chuckle at my youthful antics. I would often find myself calling Allie, concocting some elaborate excuse about staying over at a colleague's place, all the while knowing that she had figured out my little charades. A group of us would cautiously navigate our way back into Scotland Yard, doing our best to appear sober and composed, all while trying not to trip over our own two feet, which at times felt like three. If we managed to slip past the night-time security we would crash on the office floor, waking at 6 a.m., bright-eyed and bushy-tailed, ready for Saturday morning overtime.

I can't even imagine attempting such a feat now; it would surely be the end of me.

One night from that time stands out vividly. A group of us ended up at the Long Island Tearooms in Covent Garden. This was one of our go-to spots when we were ready to let loose and party the night away. Nestled down steep stairs in a basement, the bar's atmosphere was always hot and stuffy, even in winter, yet it was continuously packed. The cocktails, served in tall, chilled glasses, were dangerously enjoyable, making it easy to lose track of how many you had had.

This particular night, after drinking too many of those concoctions, I found myself dancing to 'Summer Nights' from *Grease* (it *was* the 1980s). In a moment of madness I jumped backwards onto the backs of my hands — and landed on shards of glass from a broken tumbler. A jagged edge penetrated my palm, causing excruciating pain as blood gushed out, pooling around me. Other revellers remained blissfully unaware. I tried to get to my feet but the blood made the floor slippery and I kept sliding back down.

Finally one of my friends spotted me and, thinking I had been attacked, dragged me to a wall. With a handful of toilet tissue in hand, he pulled the glass from my wound — prompting another scream from me — and wrapped my hand as best he could. At that point, the alcohol had apparently numbed my senses to the point that I felt an urge to keep dancing, even as the blood continued to flow through the 'bandaging'.

Eventually I was persuaded to get a taxi to St Thomas' Hospital Accident & Emergency, where I was kept overnight for observation. Thankfully, there was no serious damage to the tendons, and after a two-hour operation and a further day in hospital I was allowed to go home, a very angry Allie by my side.

I sometimes slept for hours on tube trains after nights of revelry, ending up in places I never knew existed. I once caught the main-line train to travel three stops to my home station and woke in Portsmouth, over a hundred kilometres away. I had to wait till 3 a.m. for a train back to London. By the time I got home I had just enough time to change out of my stinking clothes, wash, take a couple of headache tablets and get back on the train for a 7 a.m. start at Scotland Yard.

Even getting off the train at the right station didn't mean I would get home safely. I usually had my push-bike at Walton on Thames station to finish my journey home, but one night I was so drunk I completely forgot how to ride. I stood in the middle of the road, placed both feet on the pedals, and before I knew what was happening I face-planted the ground. A member of the public picked me up and dragged me to the side of the road. I told them my number and they kindly called Allie, who yet again came to my rescue.

One Saturday morning we were all gathered in the office and one of the senior staff came in looking sheepish and a bit the worse for the wear. He explained that his wife was not very happy with him after his drinking session the night before. She had woken him up as he lay on the bedroom floor and shouted: 'You were pissed last night, weren't you?'

'I may have had a couple with the lads — why?' he replied.

'I think you'd best look out the window!' she shouted back.

An official police vehicle appeared to have crashed through his neighbour's fence before grinding to a halt on his own lawn, next to the front door.

The drinking culture within the police was about to change, under the command of the new commissioner, a no-nonsense police executive who wanted to show the public that the police were professional, honest, open and transparent.

But it took a while for us to get the message. One late Friday afternoon, in the depths of The Tank, many staff members were blithely ignoring the fact that they should have been back on duty at least two hours since. The drinks were flowing and all present, including myself, were having a great time.

Without warning, about ten uniformed officers, led by a superintendent, stormed into the bar in a surprise raid on their own colleagues. They ordered everyone to put down their drinks and line up to provide names and ranks to an officer holding a clipboard.

A handful of us, me included, were escorted out and instructed to return to our offices without further incident. The focus of the raid was clearly on higher-ranking staff, the intention being to set a precedent. Two inspectors, three sergeants and several senior civilian staff were charged with conduct unbecoming of a police employee. The Tank was shut down shortly after by a commissioner determined to send a strong message.

But that wasn't quite the end of it. Each year, as Christmas approached, we transformed our offices into a festive wonderland, showcasing our creativity and camaraderie. Each team was given the freedom to design their own decorations, and we were permitted to kick off the project a full four weeks before the holiday. Our team efforts would be judged by senior personnel from the eighteenth floor, and the commissioner always seemed eager to see our creations. Our decorations grew increasingly elaborate, both in design and scale. In my fourth year I was granted the exciting opportunity to design and construct my own project, and I decided to take a rather unconventional route.

In a tongue-in-cheek homage to the now-closed bar in the basement, I envisioned building a 'Tank'. I dived head-first into this ambitious project, rallying the support of colleagues to help me gather used storage boxes, paint and other materials. Over the course of two weeks, 'The Tank' began to take shape in the office.

I may have gone a bit overboard. 'The Tank' rather dominated our office space, occupying at least a third of the room. To accommodate this we sacrificed desks and chairs. I estimated that it was about an eighth of the size of the real Tank, with its barrel reaching up to the ceiling. When the front plate was lowered, two people could fit inside comfortably.

'The Tank' became the talk of the Yard and colleagues visited to admire the spectacle. Not everyone was pleased, with management expressing concern about the work hours that must have gone into its construction. Despite this, our team felt a sense of victory at creating something so memorable. Did we win the competition? Shit yes!

My training started to incorporate a new technological advancement in the way we processed crime scenes. From the early 1990s we were getting to grips with DNA profiling, and knew this was going to be a powerful tool in solving crime. It had come a long way since it was first used in the UK to solve a murder case in 1986.

British geneticist Sir Alec Jeffreys had a 'eureka' moment in his lab in Leicester after looking at the X-ray film image of a DNA experiment in 1984. He realised the scope of DNA to identify individuals and the potential this held for crime-solving. He first put his method to use in 1985 when he was asked to confirm the relationship (if any) between a boy from Ghana and a woman in the UK who claimed to be his mother. Jeffreys obtained and analysed DNA samples from the boy, the woman and three other undisputed children already with the mother. The patterns from the DNA profiles confirmed that all four children came from the same mother.

The next test was to demonstrate the use of DNA profiling in criminal investigations, and the opportunity lay close to home for Jeffreys. In November 1983, fifteen-year-old Lynda Mann from Narborough, Leicester, had taken a shortcut on her way home from babysitting. When she failed to reach home, her parents and neighbours spent the night searching for her, but their efforts were in vain.

The following morning Lynda was discovered raped and strangled on a section of footpath locally known as 'Black Pad'. Police found semen at the crime scene and, using the forensic techniques available at the time, were able to use this to categorise the perpetrator's blood as type A. Yet despite months of investigation, they developed no additional evidence or leads, leaving the case unsolved.

In July 1986 another fifteen-year-old, Dawn Ashworth, from the neighbouring suburb of Enderby, left her home on foot to visit a friend. She was expected back by 9.30 p.m., and when she failed to return, her family called the police. Two days later she also was found raped and strangled along a footpath known as 'Ten Pound Lane', not far from where Lynda's body had been found. The MO (*modus operandi*) mirrored that of the previous case in 1983, with semen samples confirming type A blood.

A local seventeen-year-old who had learning difficulties was arrested after he demonstrated knowledge of Dawn Ashworth's body and confessed to the murder. However, he denied any involvement in the 1983 murder. The police were unable to link the suspect to Ashworth's murder and began to question the validity of his confession. It soon became evident that he was not the perpetrator.

The police approached Alec Jeffreys to assist with the investigation using his ground-breaking DNA profiling technique. He quickly determined that the semen samples collected from the two crime scenes came from the same male. In early 1987 the police requested voluntary blood samples for DNA testing from every local male aged 16–34. Despite collecting approximately five thousand samples, Jeffreys was unable to find a match for the crime samples, and the police began to lose hope of ever identifying the killer.

A breakthrough occurred when a 23-year-old man who lived outside the sampling area boasted in a pub that he had provided his blood sample in place of a colleague. He had agreed to do this for £200, as his colleague claimed to be feeling unwell at the time. This conversation was reported to the police, who arrested the man, leading him to admit that he had impersonated Colin Pitchfork.

Pitchfork had a criminal record, including convictions for indecent exposure and sexual assault. His DNA was a match for the samples from the murder scenes. In January 1988 he was sentenced to life imprisonment for the two murders.

At the time of Dawn Ashworth's murder, my partner Allie — before we met — was working in Narborough. Her sister lived in Enderby and Allie often walked down Ten Pound Lane to visit her. She was fifteen years old and she and her workmates were all interviewed by police as part of their investigation. It still sends chills down Allie's spine when we talk about it.

This double conviction was hailed as a turning point, marking a revolution in identification practices. Not only did DNA profiling identify the killer, but it also exonerated a suspect who was innocent, who could have spent the rest of his life in prison otherwise.

Alec Jeffreys continued his research to improve the DNA

amplification, allowing for greater sensitivity and automation of the profiles. It would take a few more years before the technique was ready to be used at all crime scenes. In fact the National DNA Database was not established till 1995, but by 2020 it held 6.6 million profiles.

During the initial testing phases, many senior fingerprint officers at Scotland Yard were convinced that DNA profiling was a passing trend and would eventually fade away, leaving fingerprints as the primary method of identification. How wrong they were! Today, DNA and fingerprint analysis work in harmony at crime scenes, and each plays a crucial role in identifying individuals involved in crimes and disasters. The integration of these two powerful forensic tools has significantly enhanced the accuracy and efficiency of criminal investigations.

Technology in the fingerprint section was also improving, and by my fourth year at New Scotland Yard the Automatic Fingerprint Recognition system (AFR) was beginning to advance. When I first joined, I remember a very basic computer that resembled a large suitcase, complete with a box monitor so heavy it would have been nearly impossible to steal. When you powered it on, it took at least a minute to warm up, and you'd wait in anticipation for the bold green dot to appear in the top left-hand corner of the black screen. As you typed in information, little Lego-style words danced across the screen.

At the time this system was the most advanced available, yet it only assisted with pattern recognition and conducted selected searches. It's astonishing to think that the 'floppy disks' it used each had a storage capacity of just 1.4 megabytes. The data on 771 floppy disks would add up to one gigabyte, and most of our cellphones today hold between 64 gigabytes and 1 terabyte.

By 1992 the computer screens had begun to incorporate colour, and fingerprint information was stored on more powerful hard drives. However, we were far from being able to store all eight fingers and two thumbs from one person in a way that made it easy to compare them against prints found at crime scenes. The evolution of technology in this field was just beginning, and it was exciting to think about the possibilities that lay ahead.

It was finally here: my last eight-week advanced forensic training course. Over the years, Allie had eagerly absorbed all the literature I brought home, and diligently created study notes that greatly aided my exam preparation. I firmly believe she would have excelled at the examinations herself — perhaps done better than I did.

In the four and a half years leading up to this, I had successfully completed modules on crime scene analysis, cadaver investigation, arson investigation, chemical treatments and fingerprint science. I had undergone training in disaster victim identification, court appearances and many other aspects of forensics. If I passed this last course I would step out into the streets of London to investigate real crime scenes for six months to round off my five years of training.

But they certainly saved the most challenging module for last. We had to examine mock major crime scenes, evaluating each one meticulously and obtaining all the forensic evidence that could potentially advance the investigation. We had to take comprehensive notes and photographs, and collect evidence from a scene containing a mock body, using raised stepping plates. Stepping plates are used by crime scene investigators to enable foot traffic in the area without damaging potentially crucial evidence on the floor below. The deceased then had to be preserved in a body bag and removed from the scene, whereupon we collected any weapons and gathered samples of blood, fingerprints, footwear impressions, hairs and fibres.

All this had to be achieved within a limited timeframe, despite the fact that in real-life situations time should never be a constraint when collecting evidence; you only get one shot at it. I guess they wanted to see how we operated under pressure.

Of the ten of us who embarked on this journey back in June 1988, only two decided it wasn't for them and pursued different careers. We had all endured what was reputed to be some of the toughest and most challenging forensic training offered by any police service worldwide, and here we were: still studying and, most important, still learning.

Our exams were held on the final three days of the course. As always, we had to achieve at least 80 per cent. During these last days my head was pounding with an overwhelming amount of information swirling around in that grey matter. Sleep became elusive as I would wake up with theories racing through my mind; instead of counting sheep, I found myself counting blood spatters and ridge details on fingers.

The exams over, there was little to do but wait for the results. The day stretched on and my friends and I found ourselves wandering the streets aimlessly, our conversations revolving around the exam questions. In search of a distraction we visited the local pub to calm our nerves with a drink. What started as a single pint quickly escalated, and before we knew it morning had become afternoon. With little food in our stomachs, the alcohol was coursing through our veins at an alarming rate.

We didn't have cellphones of course, and when the instructor came to the bar looking for us I knew we had overstayed our welcome. We had completely lost track of time. With our heads hung low, we made our way back to the training centre to face the moment of truth — our final course results.

There was no grand ceremony, no applause, and certainly no handshakes. Our instructor simply looked at us and said, 'All right, pissheads, you've all passed.' And just like that we were dismissed, left to process our achievement in our own hazy way.

Without a second thought we returned to the pub to continue our celebration. It all felt a bit anticlimactic, to be honest. We had worked hard, and yet our moment of triumph was overshadowed by our inebriation. Still, the excitement of what lay ahead buoyed our spirits.

As I raised my glass with my friends I felt a mixture of relief and anticipation. We had made it through the course, and now we would apply everything we had learned in the real world.

We were ready for the next phase of our journey.

Chapter 6
Investigating Crime Scenes

I had mixed emotions about leaving the fingerprint search team at New Scotland Yard. For the past four and a half years the office had served as my sanctuary — a place where I had not only honed my skills but also experienced, along with my colleagues, a sense of belonging.

I had settled comfortably into the role, and could easily see why some officers became institutionalised and resistant to change. In the office I had been surrounded by supportive colleagues who meticulously reviewed my work, ensuring every 't' was crossed and every 'i' dotted. Working at a crime scene would be starkly different. There I would be on my own, tasked with making critical decisions and knowing I had only one chance to develop and preserve the evidence before me.

Before I left, I visited the supplies section to gather the tools of the trade: police overalls, a hard hat, gloves and my personal crime scene kit. I also received personal protective gear (gloves, masks, etc.), along with a police-issue black wallet proudly displaying the silver metallic Metropolitan Police crest. I was genuinely happy: I was a kid from a council estate, and look at me now.

I was to be posted to Battersea Police Station, tasked with covering the vibrant yet challenging neighbourhoods of West London, including Brixton, Streatham and Putney. These suburbs had a reputation for car crime, burglaries and violent offences, and I knew I was in for a rollercoaster ride.

Battersea Police Station was far from being a modern facility. In fact it had a storied past, once serving as a section house for constables, and was notorious for its flooding issues — raw sewage had been known to seep into its halls, sometimes over 60 cm deep. Rebuilt in 1910, the station was a sober red-brick two-level structure, with a basement dedicated to police operations also. At the back there were seven cells. Aside from a fresh coat of paint and some updated equipment, the interior had remained largely untouched since its construction.

As I approached the front entrance on my first day I was greeted by Mel, an immaculately dressed stocky gentleman from Scotland. His deep, broad accent immediately filled the air with warmth. Mel was a highly respected SOCO in his late fifties, a veteran who had encountered every type of crime scene imaginable. He introduced me to the rest of the team, including the area commander, before leading me to a scruffy little room that would serve as my office for the foreseeable future.

Once I settled in, Mel looked me in the eye and said, 'Whatever you've learned over the years provides a sound foundation for examining crime scenes, but remember, it is not the be-all and end-all. Every crime scene is different, and each time you attend, you need to adapt to the situation at hand. Some days will be tough, and you'll see things that the public can only imagine in their worst nightmares.'

For at least two months, Mel was assigned as my chaperone, closely observing my every move and questioning each decision I made in examining crime scenes. In those early weeks I only attended 'volume' crime scenes, primarily involving car thefts and burglaries. However, Mel made the process enjoyable by sharing vivid stories from his extensive career, provoking both laughter and revulsion.

One story has remained etched in my memory. It involved a grim discovery: a person had been found hanging from the ceiling of a garage, the rope wrapped tightly around their neck and secured to the beams above. Below them, a chair lay overturned, suggesting suicide. The deceased had apparently been there for some time, as gravity had caused most of the bodily fluids to settle into their legs.

Two scene examiners arrived, initially tasked with removing the body for transport to the mortuary. They were equipped with only the most basic PPE — thin white overalls and gloves but no goggles, masks or hair nets. One of the examiners fetched a small ladder from the van and carefully positioned it next to the hanging body.

They secured insulation tape around two sections of the rope to mark where they intended to cut. Then, with a sharp blade in hand, the officer on the ladder began to slice through the rope while the other one stood underneath, ready to catch the weight of the body. Unfortunately, the blade cut through the rope much more swiftly than they had anticipated, and the body crashed to the ground before the examiner could catch it.

There was a thud and the legs of the deceased burst open, releasing a torrent of rotten bodily fluids. The unfortunate examiner below bore the brunt, and stood drenched in gooey yellow putrefied fluid. I can only imagine the horror as the fluid found its way into their hair, eyes, and even mouth. The story goes that the officer immediately began to vomit.

Get better work stories, eh?

Around 70 per cent of crime scene examiners' work anywhere in the world concerns car crime and burglary. When a stolen car was recovered, it was typically transported to a large storage facility for forensic examination before being returned to its rightful owner or the insurance company. During the early 1990s our examination protocols were somewhat limited due to time constraints. We focused mainly on fingerprint analysis, specifically on the insides and outsides of windows, with an emphasis on the driver's side. If we spotted any items inside the car that were likely introduced by the thief, we would examine those as well. The methodology was basic, but about 70 per cent of the fingerprints we developed turned out to be from the perpetrator, and many could be easily identified.

Burglaries presented us with a few more challenges. There are three distinctive types.

Opportunistic burglaries are typically spontaneous: a thief might walk down a street and notice an open window or door, allowing for easy entry without the need for force. In these cases our focus was on the point of entry. We meticulously examined the inside and outside of the open window or door to collect fingerprints. The fingerprints of someone climbing through a window tended to show specific positioning indicative of that action, so those cases were often straightforward. Doors presented us with more of a challenge, but we mainly focused on the inside opening edge where a thief might have peeked inside before entering. Generally, opportunistic burglaries resulted in minimal disturbance within the property, as the perpetrator, not knowing whether anyone was home, wanted to be in and out as fast as possible.

Professional burglaries, in contrast, are carried out by seasoned criminals who come equipped with tools to force entry. They typically use screwdrivers or jemmies, or simply smash windows to gain access. Once inside, they often cause considerable damage while searching for valuable items. Thieves operating on foot mostly target cash and jewellery. However, if they have a vehicle, usually stolen, they will often take larger items such as televisions and sound systems. I once examined a scene where a three-piece lounge suite was stolen.

This type of examination was often more time-consuming because of the volume of items of interest. Professional thieves usually wore gloves, so we had to rely on other forensic clues, such as tool marks and shoe prints.

The third distinctive type of burglary is the *insurance scam*, in which people fabricate a burglary report to the police in an attempt to claim insurance for 'stolen' items. One scene I examined involved a resident who reported that someone had broken a living-room window to steal valuable items, including a camera and jewellery, amounting to around £5000. As I examined the point of entry I noticed something unusual: all the glass shards from the broken window were outside on the grass, with very little debris inside the living room. This was a clear indication that the window had been broken from the inside. Something else caught my attention too. From marks on the carpet I could tell that the sofa had been moved from its original position directly beneath the window, presumably to ensure it wasn't damaged during the 'break-in'. Not all criminals are particularly smart . . .

Another case involved a homeowner living in squalor, who clearly owned nothing of much value. Yet this individual claimed that £50,000 worth of jewellery had been stolen from their fridge. To add insult to injury, it turned out the homeowner had taken out insurance cover the day before. The stupidity of some people amazes me.

But some scams are clever — this one almost had me fooled.

The burglary looked routine: a front door forced with minimal damage, rooms ransacked, valuables missing. Out back, the kitchen window was open, with scuff marks on the worktop.

I lifted several fingerprints from inside, then found more on the bottom edge of the kitchen window frame, pointing outward — classic 'exit' prints. The homeowner denied climbing out but grew uneasy when I asked for his prints to eliminate him from the scene.

Back at the station, I matched his prints to those on the window. Confronted, he admitted staging the burglary to cover his mounting debts. The case was cracked by one detail — the direction of the fingerprints.

My confidence grew, and after four weeks of closely chaperoning me, Mel pretty much left me to myself. The six months flew by. By June 1993 I had successfully completed my five years' training and was duly signed off by Scotland Yard as a certified fingerprint expert and crime scene examiner.

My next four years' service would involve examining all types of crime scene throughout London, including complex and more serious incidents.

Arson scenes were among the most challenging. They were dirty and intricate crimes to examine, but I loved nothing more. Over my decade in the field with the Metropolitan Police I found immense satisfaction in uncovering the causes and origins of fires.

In London, any intentional fire falls under the jurisdiction of the police to examine and investigate. I would arrive at the scene equipped with my specialised arson kit, including PPE and a case containing items to gather and preserve items that may contain an accelerant.

Arson scenes vary greatly in complexity. A simple scenario might involve someone pouring fuel through the letter slot in the front door and igniting it. I would photograph the damage and document the burn patterns on the door and floor, noting how the liquid fuel behaved upon contact. I would then take carpet samples for laboratory analysis to ascertain the type of fuel used.

More complex scenarios involved buildings or vehicles that had been completely consumed by flames, leaving little intact. Here the scene investigation is like assembling a large three-dimensional jigsaw puzzle. I would start by photographing the damage, being mindful that the fire brigade's efforts to extinguish the blaze will have caused additional damage. My goal was then to restore the scene as far as possible to its original state before the fire. I would remove charred debris while looking for protected areas of walls and flooring that might have escaped damage. Then I would search for fuel pattern marks on the floor, as these can often point to the fire's origin. In some circumstances I might measure the depth of charring on wooden frames to help determine the intensity and direction of heat exposure. After gathering any available data, I would photograph the reconstructed area, before collecting samples for further scientific analysis.

I had completed my first year in the field and the most serious crime scenes I had attended alone were robberies. I had shadowed senior officers during a couple of murder investigations, observing and learning from their expertise. On rare occasions I was tasked with fingerprinting a few items to assist in their examinations, but my involvement was limited.

One morning, as I started my duty at 7.30 a.m., that changed. The duty inspector rushed into my office and said, 'There's been a murder and we need someone to examine the scene immediately.' The reason for the rush was that it was on a public highway, and the weather was expected to worsen. I was still in Battersea and my mentor, Mel, was away on one of his exotic holidays, leaving me without my go-to guide.

I quickly began calling other stations for assistance, but each time I was met with the same frustrating response: 'Sorry, pal, we already have a murder on our patch and we have no one spare.' It was one of those chaotic London days in which everything seemed to happen at once. Multiple incidents were unfolding and there were not enough qualified personnel to attend them all.

After I'd spent about an hour on the phone, one of the senior examiners called me back to authorise me to attend the scene in Battersea. His final words of encouragement were: 'Don't fuck it up, Coyle.'

I took a deep breath and composed myself before heading to the forensic storeroom. I loaded my arms with supplies, cramming everything into the back of the small police van. With my heart racing, I set off towards the crime scene.

Ten minutes later I reached the scene and saw four police cars blocking the road. Yellow police cordon tape flapped in the breeze, securing the area. I parked the van at the edge of the cordon, and before I could even step out of the vehicle a uniformed officer approached me and began to relay the details of the incident. Then he paused mid-flight. 'Are you the only one coming?' Another confidence-booster — just what I needed. Without replying, I opened the rear of the van and methodically began to dress myself in full PPE. Once I was suited up, I grabbed my all-important notebook and pen and made my way to the crime scene.

I was relieved to see a detective already present, waiting to brief me. He explained that a person had been stabbed during a fight in an alleyway. The victim had staggered up the walkway and collapsed in the street, where a passer-by found him and called an ambulance. The paramedics arrived promptly, providing assistance before rushing the victim to hospital, but he died en route.

I didn't know whether to feel relieved or disappointed. It was my first murder scene and there was no body in situ to examine. The detective reassured me that the alleyway had been preserved, and the street was cordoned off at the point where the victim had collapsed. The crime scene photographer had already been and gone.

My first task was to survey the scene and note any items of interest. I had to tread carefully, ensuring I didn't step on anything that could provide valuable evidence. My examination included the surrounding area, and I walked slowly up and down the alley, my eyes peeled for clues. I found nothing obvious — no weapon helpfully dropped by the suspect as they fled.

At the entrance of the alleyway two metallic tubular rails protruded partway over the footpath to slow people on bikes or skateboards. On one side of the concrete path was a wooden fence approximately 2 metres high that ran the length of the 30-metre alleyway, and on the other side was a fence of green wire mesh. About two metres beyond the rails I saw the start of a trail of blood drips that continued all the way down to where the victim had collapsed. A large pool of blood had formed at that point, and scattered about were the remnants of the ambulance personnel's efforts — bandages and other items used in their attempt to save the victim's life.

I returned to the van for my silver forensic case and made my way back to the beginning of the alleyway. Inside the case was an array of essential tools: fingerprint powder, various brushes, a torch, casting tools, fingerprint tape, plastic backing sheets, and cotton swabs for sampling blood. And yes, there was an iconic Sherlock Holmes-style magnifying glass.

The tubular rails were the ideal place for me to start my fingerprint examination — far enough from the blood drops, with the wind blowing favourably to ensure no powder drifted onto the drops. The Met commonly used aluminium powder, a choice that raised concerns in many countries due to its potential health risks. Nevertheless, it was a staple in my forensic toolkit at the time. I applied the powder to the railings and, using my torch and magnifying glass, scanned for any signs of friction (raised) ridge detail. Several fingers and palm prints emerged, clearly defined against the surface. I marked each with a small arrow and recorded their descriptions, locations and measurements in my notebook.

People often picture fingerprints as perfectly formed impressions, each one neatly separated and easy to read. But in real life, prints often overlap and merge. In those cases, we preserve them exactly as they are and send them back to the fingerprint section, whose job is to untangle the puzzle and figure out which fingers belong to whom.

Naturally, precision is paramount in forensic work, especially when it comes to measurements. Establishing a reference point from which to record all measurements not only maintained clarity but also prevented any confusion if you later had to recount your actions in a court of law.

I used the specialist tape to preserve the developed prints, pressing firmly to ensure the powder adhered. I smoothly pulled the tape away from the substrate at a 45-degree angle and placed it carefully onto a plastic backing sheet. The final and crucial step was labelling the evidence. I attached an exhibit label across the tape and backing sheet and carefully recorded the date, location and exhibit number.

Once I had secured all eight fingerprint lifts in an envelope, I took a moment to rub the area where the prints had developed, to ensure that any ridge detail residue was destroyed. This is an essential practice at every crime scene. Otherwise, if there is another crime investigation at the same location, examiners may inadvertently collect the older prints.

My attention now turned to the blood. The trail consisted of small drops of 'passive' blood — where the blood has dripped from the victim after injury and landed on the ground to form circular droplets with tiny spikes around the edges. I concluded that the passive blood drops came from a single individual, so I only needed to capture a representative sample. For a scene like this, I would typically aim for around ten samples.

However, this was my first murder scene and I wasn't taking any risks — I sampled every single drop of blood I saw. By the time I finished, I had around 40 samples, completely exhausting the stock of swabs in the van. I then documented every single one in my notes, which was transforming from a straightforward log into something resembling a novel.

I was preparing to hand the scene back to the investigating team when something caught my eye. At the beginning of the blood trail I noticed that the wooden fence panelling was broken in several places. This could easily have been attributed to normal wear and tear in a busy public alleyway, but upon closer inspection I saw that the fence appeared quite new. I decided to request the removal of the damaged panel for a detailed examination back at the station. I explained to the officer how they should handle the item and left them to it.

Back at Battersea Police Station I wrote up my reports and submissions. Within a couple of hours a lorry pulled up at the back security gate. An officer approached my office and asked, 'Where do you want all the fence panels?'

I was bemused. 'Don't you mean fence *panel* singular?'

'I think it's best if you come to the rear yard,' he replied.

I followed him outside where, to my astonishment, I saw a large truck filled with around fifteen fence panels, all neatly lined up and awaiting unloading. The truck driver stood by — he had been told not to unload the panels until instructed to do so, as they required a forensic examination.

I stood there in disbelief — this had to be some kind of prank.

It turned out the officer at the scene had misheard my initial request. He had donned protective gear and pulled off every single fencing panel. Apparently the alleyway looked as if it had been robbed in broad daylight and the council office was none too happy. I assisted with the unloading and, after removing the one panel I needed, requested that the rest be returned to the scene and restored to their rightful place.

I submitted the fingerprints to New Scotland Yard and within a couple of days I heard that the team had successfully identified two individuals from those prints. One of them had already been on the radar as a potential suspect, so the fingerprint evidence was what they needed to progress their investigation. That suspect was ultimately charged with murder and later found guilty. As the fingerprints had been deposited in a public place, that evidence alone was not enough to implicate them directly, but was enough to place them at the scene.

Chapter 7
Jumped or Pushed?

It was 7.30 a.m. and I was at my desk, organising the day's workload. I was set to examine six crimes that had come in overnight: three burglaries, two car crimes and a theft from a shop. Just as I prepared to call the victims of these crimes, my police radio sprang to life with a message that an incident had just been reported at a block of flats in the Clapham area. A member of the public had called in to report that someone had fallen from one of the upper floors and landed in the public stairwell below. Police were on their way.

Should I wait for more information or continue with my scheduled cases? I wondered. Ultimately, I left the office and headed to the first burglary scene. I'd decided against calling the victim for now; I wanted to remain flexible in case I was called away to assist with the unfolding situation in Clapham. As I navigated London traffic I tuned into the police radio chatter, a constant hum that often faded into the background. However, certain keywords managed to pierce the noise: SOCO, death, murder. Then I heard an officer's voice repeat, 'Is there any SOCO on duty in the area?'

I pulled my van over and responded. 'Charlie Tango 22, can I assist with your call?'

'If that's the SOCO, can you assist us with a serious crime scene?' the officer replied.

At that point I'd been in the job for a couple of years and assisted in multiple murders so I was confident to deal with this request.

I manoeuvred through the relentless traffic and made it to the scene within fifteen minutes. As I approached the block of flats I saw a cluster of six marked police vehicles parked haphazardly along the street nearby. I made my way to the gated entrance to the building, where a police officer on duty recognised me and opened the gate. I was met by a member of the investigative team, who pulled me aside to brief me on the details they had gathered so far.

He told me a deceased person was lying in the building's enclosed stairway, which had been secured for the investigation. The individual had fallen from the eighteenth floor through a communal hallway skylight.

'We're unsure whether they were pushed out the window or they jumped.'

'Why do you think they might have been pushed?' I asked.

'We've been approached by a member of the public who was in their flat on the eighteenth floor. They reported hearing an intense argument between two people, followed by screams, then silence.'

'I see.' I nodded.

'We have a person assisting us with our inquiries, but we need you to examine the body and the window on the eighteenth floor to ascertain what happened.'

I returned to the van to gather my equipment and change into PPE.

Before examining the window I wanted to see the location of the deceased. The block of flats was part of a new private estate designed to attract affluent Londoners to the borough. It stood twenty storeys high, with a private gated entrance that offered residents secure parking. The small garden areas, complete with park benches, created an illusion of tranquillity, allowing residents to relax and forget they were in the bustling heart of London.

To the right of the main lift was a fire door that led to concrete steps all the way up to the top floor. The door currently bore the unmistakeable 'Crime Scene Do Not Cross' tape, and a uniformed police officer stood in front. He opened the door for me and I saw around ten concrete steps leading to the first landing, where I gathered the body lay.

I examined these steps for clues. Then I walked up, keeping to the right of the stairwell to maintain a single clear pathway for both entering and leaving the scene, and saw the deceased person lying on their front on the landing between staircases. There was blood spatter up the wall, consistent with arterial-style spraying, indicating that a main artery had been severed. The person was wearing a blue top that was partly pulled up to expose the skin on their back, and a pink jacket was scrunched above the shoulders and covered the head area. To the left of the body, blood was pooling from the head to the waist, and on the other side of the body was more arterial blood.

The victim was dressed in jeans, but both legs had been severed cleanly below the knees, leaving only a small section of flesh visible at the calf. A black boot lay discarded in one corner of the landing, with part of a denim-clad leg emerging from it, and the lower part of the fibula bone protruded through the fabric. Just around the corner, resting on the second step, a second boot mirrored the first.

The landing was littered with shards of glass, and as I looked up, the source of the glass became apparent. Above me was a domed glass ceiling covering the stairwell landing. A metal partition ran down the centre, and three of the six glass frames had shattered where the victim had fallen through. Their lower limbs must have been severed on impact with the frame.

Interesting, I thought, that only the legs had suffered this fate. Then I carefully lifted the pink jacket slightly away from the shoulders and saw, to my horror, that there was no head.

At this point the lead investigator called up to me. 'Tom, we've found a head in the carpark.'

'Yep,' I shouted back. 'I have just noticed the body is missing one.'

We both left the building and made our way to the carpark,

where he pointed to a white car with blood on the bonnet. They were assuming the head had bounced off it. The investigator led me to a lowered walkway below the carpark, and in a corner I saw a mass of black hair. I walked around and the person's face stared right back at me. Nothing prepares you for this sort of thing, and I got a hell of a shock. We covered the head with a clean cloth provided by the ambulance crew, and set up another scene guard to protect the area.

I returned to the main lobby, my trusty silver crime scene case in hand. This time I took the lift to the eighteenth floor. When the lift doors slid open I was met by another uniformed officer, who was tasked with securing the landing and the window through which it was believed the victim had fallen (or been pushed). The window was a large, metal-framed single pane attached to the main structure by two swing hinges. Below the window, a plastic panel extended all the way to the concrete floor.

Think for a moment about what you would be doing with your hands if you were being pushed out that window. Instinctively you would try to grab the window frame to stop yourself going through the opening. The same goes for your feet — you would place your soles or the edges of your shoes firmly against the wall or the frame to lock yourself in place.

If this happened, then an examination of the frame and wall with fingerprint powders and brushes would show up numerous finger and palm prints. The fingers may be angled to two o'clock and ten o'clock from the hands reaching out. There would be a significant number of fingerprint impressions all around the frame from where you clung on for dear life. Shoe impressions would likely be visible, as well as scuffs on the wall under the window, and maybe even on the bottom of the window frame.

During my examination I found no evidence of this type of movement. What I did develop was four sets of fingerprints of the right fore, mid and ring fingers. Two sets were from the right hand, deposited on the inside surface of the left-hand side of the frame (as viewed from the inside), and the other two sets, from the left hand, were on the right-hand side of the frame. All the prints were oriented outwards, towards the internal wall, consistent with somebody standing on the ledge outside the window, facing inwards towards the landing and holding the frame, perhaps arguing with someone on the inside.

I discovered two further sets of right-hand prints on the bottom of the frame, just off-centre, one set pointing straight down towards the floor and the other set pointing to around eight o'clock, consistent with somebody climbing out of the window.

Outside the window there was a dusty ledge that had accumulated grime over the years. Within the dust and grime I found impressions of footwear with the toe area pointing towards the wall. The pattern was characteristic of work-style boots.

I quickly contacted the police photographer, who was

fortunately still on site, to record all these impressions, then I preserved the fingerprints. It being the eighteenth floor, I decided against climbing out the window to preserve the footwear impressions, hoping the photos would provide sufficient detail, which they did.

There was a footwear impression of the same block-style pattern on the concrete floor beneath the window, composed of dust particles. Traditional methods like powders and brushes are not effective in such cases, so I used an electrostatic lifting device (ESLD) to preserve the impression. First you photograph the impression. Then you take a special metallic film, silver on one side and black on the other, and place it black-side down over the impression. You connect the ESLD to the film with a lead and apply an electrostatic charge, which attracts and lifts the dust particles onto the film. When you remove the film you see the footwear impression on the black side.

I erased all ridge detail from the site, packed up my equipment and went down in the lift to tell the investigating officer I had completed my examination on the eighteenth floor. Based on the evidence I had gathered, I said, it was my professional opinion that the individual had climbed out of the window voluntarily onto the ledge. There was no indication of foul play.

In the early 1990s it was standard operating procedure for a doctor to pronounce the person dead at the scene before we could preserve the body and transport it to the mortuary for a PM. The doctor was often running late and all we could do was wait. When the doctor finally arrived on this occasion, we were all amazed when he went straight to the head in the walkway. He removed the cover and placed two fingers on the remaining part of the neck trying to locate a pulse. The investigator and I glanced at each other and rolled our eyes in amazement. After 30 seconds the doctor got to his feet and said, 'I can confirm that this person is dead.' No shit, Sherlock. Apparently the doctor had to prove they had complied with correct procedure or they could lose the £50 they received for the death certificate.

The head was placed in a sterile white plastic bag for the pathologist. The lead investigator and I then returned to the landing and bagged the body and feet.

The investigating team talked to the partner of the deceased, who had been heard arguing with them before the incident, and provided a credible explanation for why the person decided to end their own life.

By this point in my career I had been in the job for twelve years and had attended and examined thousands of crime scenes of all types and not much seemed to faze me. I had witnessed first hand the sheer variety and brutality of human behaviour and the depths to which an individual could sink to inflict harm on another.

I was now based in Twickenham, a picturesque suburb of London and markedly different from the chaotic heart of the city. With its leafy streets and strong sense of community,

Twickenham was populated by those fortunate few who could afford the high house prices and rents. Unlike the bustling centre of London, where people hurried about their lives, often oblivious to one another, Twickenham exuded a welcoming charm. Residents exchanged friendly greetings in the street, no doubt grateful to be living in a neighbourhood where the fear of random acts of violence was significantly diminished.

My office in Feltham was a modern, clean, fresh space, a welcome change from the cramped environment of Battersea. I worked alongside two SOCOs, and while they were dispatched to attend to burglaries and car thefts, I remained on standby for serious crimes.

At nine o'clock one overcast morning I was enjoying my first cup of coffee when the phone rang. After the customary greetings the area inspector said, 'I need you to examine an address in Shepperton. It's a murder scene and it's quite unusual.' He had my full attention as he continued. 'We had a call this morning around 5.30 from a man who said he had killed his wife and was waiting in the living room for us to arrest him. We've taken him into custody, and responding officers have located a body in the bedroom. Would you please attend.'

I arranged to meet the investigating team and photographer at the scene in the next 30 minutes.

I ensured that my van was stocked with the necessary equipment and set off for the property, hoping the rain would hold off and that most of the work to be done would be inside.

Officers were already conducting door-to-door inquiries,

gathering information from neighbours. I parked my vehicle and kitted up in the mandatory PPE before making my way up the concrete driveway with my notebook and pen. The house was a semi-detached, two-storey structure, featuring an inbuilt garage and a porch. I met the lead investigator who told me a woman's body was in the upstairs main bedroom, and the scene had been secured after an initial search. The husband was in custody and had confessed to the crime.

As I stepped through the front door I was met by a familiar face, the police photographer.

'Morning, Tom,' he said. 'I'm just finishing up downstairs and I'll follow you upstairs to the main scene when you're ready.' Then he added, 'By the way, I noticed some blood on a phone in the study while I was walking around.'

The layout of the downstairs was straightforward, consisting of a long hallway leading to the kitchen, a study, and a dining area that also served as an office. The living room was at the rear of the property and the curtains were still drawn. What caught my attention immediately were two sofas that were covered in bedding, suggesting someone had slept there the previous night.

In the study I saw the landline phone which, as the photographer had mentioned, bore signs of blood. With a closer look I could see ridge detail.

With my initial observations made downstairs, including checking the doors and windows for any obvious signs of forced entry, I made my way upstairs with the photographer. We found the main bedroom, three smaller bedrooms and a combined toilet and bathroom. It was evident that two of the smaller bedrooms belonged to children, while the third was cluttered with various household items including a vacuum cleaner, an ironing board and an iron.

On the landing was a dog basket filled with old towels, indicating that a pet was also part of this household.

We stepped into the main bedroom and the atmosphere shifted. The curtains were still closed. A woman's body was lying on its back on the bed, her top half covered by the duvet. Two pillows rested beneath her head, one of which was folded over the top of the head. Just below the pillows, on top of the duvet, lay a metal hammer with a black rubber handle, and it was unmistakeably stained with blood.

The bedding below the pillows was soaked with blood right through to the mattress. Blood spatter adorned the wall above the bed and a set of drawers, and continued as far as the wall beneath the drawn curtains. There were indications of bone and brain matter mixed within the spatter, some of which had travelled a fair distance.

The photographer set about recording every detail, paying special attention to the body and the blood spatter. We then pulled back the pillow covering the victim's head, and it was a gruesome sight. Serious injuries had occurred mainly to the top and left side of the head, with large chunks of the skull missing, and brain matter scattered about nearby. Her right eye was closed while the left eye remained open, its gaze fixed directly ahead. The eyelid was missing, and thick crimson-coloured blood was smeared across much of that side of the face.

Given that we had a suspect in custody, you might assume that this would be a straightforward case that did not require exhaustive scene examination. However, every serious crime scene demands a thorough investigation. It's crucial to gather as much information as possible, as narratives can change over time. Confessions can be redacted, and other evidence can come to light further down the track. Once the scene is released back to the family, there's no returning for a second go at collecting critical evidence.

While I was waiting for the all-clear from the photographer, I took another tour of the house to make sure there was nothing I had overlooked the first time. Then I began my examination of the scene.

I first focused on the hammer. It was clear from the wounds inflicted that this was the weapon used. The hammer could provide significant information, including cross-matching to the wounds on the victim's head, blood transfer from the victim, and to the fingerprints of the suspect. Bloody fingerprints from the suspect are one of the best pieces of evidence you can obtain from a murder scene.

To ensure the hammer was transported safely to the laboratory, I used a pre-cut exhibit box. This would not only protect the item but also prevent any alteration during transit. Handling any evidence that requires multiple examinations is always challenging, with the ongoing risk of cross-contamination. So, with gloved hands I placed my right thumb and forefinger on the shaft beneath the hammer head, ensuring I was supporting it securely. With my left forefinger I held the bottom tip of the handle. This method not only provides a firm grip but also minimises contact with areas that might have been touched by the suspect. I then secured the hammer inside the box using sterilised garden wire, which experience had shown to be both effective and reliable. I took a moment to document the process.

My next step was to observe and document the blood spatter. In a more complex scenario, where multiple blood spatter patterns indicated movements between different areas, I would have requested the assistance of a blood spatter expert from the laboratory. But in this case the situation was more straightforward. The scene was confined to a single part of one room and I was confident in my ability to analyse and describe the size, shape and distribution patterns of the blood spatter.

It became abundantly clear that the blood on the walls and drawers had resulted from the forceful impact of the hammer striking the victim's skull. This type of blood spatter is known as impact spatter, and it differs significantly from the 'passive' blood drops I had encountered at the murder scene I described in Chapter 6.

The stains in this room were elongated, featuring a pointed end that indicated the direction from which the blood had originated. The thin tail end of each stain pointed away from the impact site, revealing the trajectory of the blood as it splattered across the surfaces. This analysis not only helps to reconstruct the events leading up to the tragedy but also provides valuable insight into the level of violence. I also confirmed the presence of pieces of brain and skull on the walls, the floor and the drawers.

After examining the blood spatter, I took a moment to survey the area for any additional evidence that might aid the investigation. Satisfied that I had captured all relevant details, I moved to the bathroom to inspect the sink for signs of blood. It's common for suspects to wash their hands to eliminate any traces of evidence. I examined the taps for bloodstained fingerprints and swabbed all surfaces, including the plug and plug hole, to collect samples for further analysis by the laboratory.

As I continued my search, I discovered a pile of clothing in one of the bedrooms that showed clear indications of blood staining. I carefully bagged the items individually and labelled them with their relevant exhibit numbers. These would also be examined by specialists at the laboratory.

I had reached the point where we could safely remove the deceased without the risk of contaminating other evidence. This task fell to the lead investigator and me. I got a large white plastic sheet used as a body bag, three smaller bags and some tape from my van. We secured two of the smaller bags over the victim's hands to preserve any potential evidence, including fingernail samples and ridge detail.

Next, we faced the delicate task of bagging the head, including as much as possible of the loose skull and brain matter. The investigator carefully clasped his hands around the head to stabilise it while I positioned the bag. We were moving as slowly and carefully as we could, but as we manoeuvred, the head shifted slightly, causing the left eyeball to dislodge and roll over the cheek, heading directly towards me. I dropped the bag and managed to catch the eyeball just before it rolled off the bed and onto the floor. I gently placed it back in the eye socket. When the head was secured in the bag, we taped it tightly to ensure everything was securely contained.

The final step involved lifting the body onto the opened plastic sheet, then carefully folding over the edges and taping both ends securely. Using the rolling gurney from the undertaker's van we wheeled the body from the house and loaded it, trying our best to ensure the integrity of the evidence and the dignity of the deceased throughout. The body was then transported to the mortuary to await a post-mortem.

I then went to examine the bloodstained phone in the study, which sat on an antique-style writing table. Fingerprint stains in blood can be notoriously difficult to detect with the naked eye. Typically, forensic investigators rely on chemical treatments to enhance the visibility and contrast of the ridge detail. A chemical called amido black (and there were others, dependent on background colour) was applied to the surface — the phone in this instance. The chemical would bind to the proteins present in blood (and other bodily fluids), producing a distinctive blue-black stain that made fingerprints more visible.

After applying the chemical and rinsing the surface, clear ridge details were revealed. I labelled the developed finger and palm prints to enable the photographer, who was still on site, to record images of the prints using a macro lens to ensure high-quality documentation.

My final area of examination was the living room, where my objective was to look for any items bearing post-event blood staining. I'd been told the suspect sat on a sofa while waiting for the police, so I examined the immediate surroundings. On the coffee table I saw a cigarette packet with faint blood staining, as well as a coffee mug. From these two items I developed an additional three fingerprints, which I added to my collection of exhibits.

Before I left the scene I had a debrief with members of the investigation team and heard details of the husband's confession. He told police he and his wife had gone out the previous night to socialise with friends. Both had consumed a significant amount of alcohol, which contributed to the escalation of tensions when they returned home. An argument erupted, during which the wife admitted that for over six months she had been having an affair with one of the friends present at the party. Following this revelation she went to bed while the husband remained downstairs. Overwhelmed by anger and jealousy, he eventually snapped, went to the shed to get a hammer and used it to strike his wife multiple times in her sleep.

The following morning I was at the mortuary, dressed in fresh PPE, preparing to assist the pathologist with the forensic examination of the body. As usual, I was immediately hit by the familiar musty smell of the place — it's a scent that is genuinely hard to articulate.

The cadaver lay on a metal gurney, still wrapped in the plastic sheeting we had used at the crime scene. The photographer who had documented the scene was with me, ready to capture detailed images of the injuries. This was most easily done from above, with the body on the mortuary floor, so we carefully opened both ends of the plastic sheeting, and removed the bags covering the hands and head. Then we lifted the plastic with the body on it, and lowered it to the floor. The sheeting was large — 3 metres by 4 metres — allowing ample space around the body to prevent cross-contamination. The small bags were placed in exhibit bags for separate examination later if required.

Blood from the head wounds was oozing onto the sheeting, pooling behind the head. The deceased was dressed only in a pair of white underwear, so there was not much clothing to remove. Her hands were placed gently on her chest and the photographer set up his tripod and got to work. Soon, we needed to turn the body over so he could photograph the back. This was particularly challenging because of the extensive skull damage, but with careful coordination between the pathologist, the pathologist's assistant and myself, we managed. As we did, more dark blood flowed from the large wound on the left side of her head, a clear indication of the severity of the injuries. At the crime scene the blood had not only soaked through to the bedding and mattress but had also spread down to the victim's leg area, and now the back of her underwear was soaked in blood. The injuries had caused substantial blood loss.

Parts of her body had a bluish discoloration, due to blood

pooling inside the body from the effect of gravity. This natural occurrence is called livor mortis, or lividity — when the heart stops pumping, blood settles to the lowest parts of the body.

Once the photographer had completed the general shots, we lifted the body back onto the gurney and removed the white plastic sheeting (placing it in an exhibit bag).

The pathologist now began the PM, searching first for any additional injuries sustained during the assault. It quickly became evident that the left hand had absorbed one of the hammer blows. Her wedding and engagement rings were severely flattened, and discoloured areas on the middle finger and knuckles indicated bruising consistent with defence wounds. We noted similar discoloration on the middle finger of the right hand. These passive defence wounds strongly indicated that the victim was conscious during the initial stages of the assault.

To determine the full extent of injury, the pathologist cleaned the head wound and cleared away blood. Just above the left eye lay an orbital fracture measuring about 10 cm by 4 cm. After he had carefully returned the displaced tissue and shaved the area for visibility, a pattern became clear: multiple blows had split the scalp and fractured the skull, each leaving a curved impression consistent with a hammer. The severity was obvious — any single blow could have been fatal. In total, the pathologist recorded over twenty impact sites.

The pathologist completed the PM by looking to see if there were any underlying issues that may have caused death, eventually concluding that death was caused by the hammer blows.

Back at New Scotland Yard, the fingerprints developed from the hammer, phone, cigarette packet and coffee mug were all identified as belonging to the husband. The blood staining found on his clothing was consistent with someone who had been in close proximity to the attack when it occurred. The remaining swabs were retained for potential future analysis.

The husband pleaded guilty in court and was sentenced to life in prison.

One day a visibly distressed woman entered the police station and approached the front counter with an alarming confession. She claimed that there was a dead body in a nearby flat and insisted that she and four of her friends were responsible.

The woman was quickly ushered into an interview room, where a detective from CID went to talk to her. She recounted a chaotic scene. There had been six people present, she said, all heavily intoxicated and under the influence of drugs. Without any warning, one man had suddenly attacked another man with his fists, inciting the others to join in the assault. She described a frenzied attack lasting about ten minutes, during which the victim was subjected to a brutal beating with various weapons. After the assault, the woman said they wrapped the victim's body in a rug and fled the scene, forming a pact among themselves to never speak of the incident.

However, burdened by guilt, about five days later she felt compelled to come forward and report what had happened, so that the victim could be laid to rest.

I received a call from CID and made my way to the flat along with the lead investigator and another officer. The flat was on the second floor, and it struck me as odd that no one from the complex had reported any unusual odours emanating from it. The door itself was a solid white UPVC model equipped with secure bolts, and unfortunately we had no keys. However, anticipating this problem, we had a locksmith on standby. We cautioned him that it might smell pretty bad inside. When the locksmith opened the door we were taken aback to find that there was no foul smell at all. In fact the air was filled with a pleasant aroma of fresh linen . . .

In the living room it was clear from the disarray that a party had taken place. Bottles were strewn across the floor and furniture. A wooden coffee table was covered with drug paraphernalia: lines of white powder, spoons with remnants of heroin. Discarded plastic baggies and crumpled tinfoil littered the floor. Two ashtrays overflowed with cigarette butts and hand-rolled cigarettes.

As we surveyed the mess we exchanged glances, and almost in unison voiced our surprise: 'There's no body in here.' Just as I was starting to question the woman's report, my attention was drawn to a rolled-up rug at the far end of the room. Lined up beside the rug were eight bottles of deodorising spray. It appeared that someone had returned to the scene and poured the fragrant liquid over the rug and surrounding floor to mask whatever unpleasant odour was cocooned in the rug itself. The deodorising spray had done such an effective job, I have been a loyal customer of the product ever since, to get rid of odours at home (though not from dead bodies, I hasten to add!)

At this point we needed to call in a photographer to record everything before we investigated what lay wrapped within the rug. The photographer arrived after about 30 minutes and set to work, manoeuvring his tripod and camera to capture every angle and detail. About twenty minutes later we were cleared to continue the scene search.

The lead investigator and I prepared ourselves to unroll the rug. It turned out to be only about 2 metres long, but inside was another, similar rug. We paused a moment to allow the photographer to document this. Then we grabbed the edges of the second rug and began to unroll it. Inside it was a sleeping bag soaked in blood. The top was bound tightly with a toggle. 'How long is this going on for?' the lead investigator muttered. 'It's like a morbid game of pass the parcel.'

At this point an unmistakable odour began to permeate the room, one that was familiar to all of us — the stench of death. The deodorising spray had no chance against this, and we paused for a moment, allowing our senses to adjust.

I finally managed to loosen the toggle and slowly pulled back the hooded portion of the bag, while the lead investigator unzipped the side.

It was a horrific sight. Inside lay the body of a slim male, dressed in a torn T-shirt that was soaked in blood. His trousers were unzipped and wrapped around his ankles. It was evident that the assault had been not only brutal but prolonged. The severity of the injuries made it impossible to identify the victim from his face. Blood masked his features. His nose was broken, his eyes were swollen tightly shut, and shallow cuts scored his forehead. On the upper left, the skull was noticeably flattened, consistent with a forceful strike to the head.

There were about twenty stab wounds to the chest, and defensive cuts and abrasions on the victim's hands. Bruises to the abdomen area, some resembling footwear impressions, suggested he had been stomped or kicked. There were also injuries to his genital area. This murder was clearly a frenzied attack by a mob under the heavy influence of drugs and alcohol, as the woman had reported.

After the photographer had documented all the injuries we bagged the body and handed it off to the undertaker. Examining and recording the crime scene would occupy me for the rest of the day — and then some. I needed to thoroughly search every corner of the flat for fingerprints, footwear impressions and DNA samples.

My initial task involved collecting DNA samples, to prevent any risk of cross-contamination with other examinations I conducted. Since the establishment of the UK National DNA Database in 1995 we routinely collected DNA samples at crime scenes, using sterilised cotton swabs. Physical items such as cigarette butts also provided DNA profiles, so I preserved the butts from the two ashtrays in exhibit bags and sealed them securely. There were blood marks on the carpet so I cut out the affected areas and placed each piece of carpet in a separate bag. Given that it was impossible to determine which person had drunk from which bottle, I collected samples from all 35 liquor bottles at the scene.

I then turned to developing footwear impressions from the smooth linoleum floor surfaces in the kitchen and bathroom. In most cases, like fingerprints, footwear impressions are latent (not visible to the naked eye) and need to be developed, unless a contaminant is present on the sole (blood, oil, dirt). The process was relatively straightforward: I applied a carbon-based black powder to an area of floor using a brush made from squirrel hair. With gentle sweeping motions I brushed the floor until the outline of the footwear sole began to emerge. At this point I could apply additional powder to enhance the contrast and clarity of the impression, taking care not to overbrush or apply too much powder, which can degrade the impression.

The only footwear impressions I was developing were from trainers, so I concentrated instead on impressions of bare feet that were also developing with the treatment. To do this I used carbon powder and large gel-like sheets. I placed the sheets over the impressions to attract the carbon powder used in the development process, and the gel sheets captured the impressions, which I preserved by placing clear plastic over them.

I collected fibre samples from various parts of the rugs that were around the body, as well as hair and fibre samples from the backs of sofas and chairs. For this I patted the area with a roll of specially designed low-adhesive tape. The tape was then placed on a large piece of plastic sheeting to preserve the samples. I recorded the exact areas from which each sample was taken.

My final job was to develop fingerprints. I inspected all potential sources, including the bottles I had already sampled for DNA, doors, kitchen utensils, and areas in the bathroom and bedroom. By the end I had preserved about 40 finger and palm prints from a variety of surfaces. I also bagged a large cast-iron griddle pan that had blood stains on its surface, and all the tinfoil from the coffee table and the floor for fingerprint analysis in the laboratory.

The tinfoil would undergo a chemical treatment known as cyanoacrylate (CNA) fuming, commonly referred to as superglue fuming. The exhibit is placed in a sealed chamber inside which the CNA is placed in a silver aluminium container above a heating element. The CNA is heated to 120°C, causing it to evaporate. As it does so, it polymerises on any latent fingerprints present, transforming them from translucent to white, making them more visible. Once the glue has adhered to the item, it's possible to either apply powder to enhance the now-visible prints or use another chemical dye to further highlight the ridge detail. This process is used throughout the world to recover fingerprints from all types of non-porous surface.

Despite the flat in question being only a one-bedroom unit, the scene examination was very time-consuming, with a lot of evidence to gather. TV crime shows portray scene examiners casually waving a brush over a surface as if they were dusting for cleanliness, suggesting that an extensive scene investigation can be completed in about an hour. The reality is quite different. In this instance, the examination took at least ten hours. It was exhausting work.

The following morning I drove to New Scotland Yard to personally deliver the fingerprint lifts to the fingerprint murder team, who promptly began analysing them. Later that day I met with the lead investigator, who told me the suspect who had come in to confess the previous day had named two other people allegedly present during the incident, and they were looking for them.

We reviewed the evidence and agreed to send the tinfoil and the cast-iron pan to the fingerprint laboratory for chemical treatment. Additionally, I would submit a random selection of DNA swabs from the bottles, along with the carpet samples, to the laboratory for profiling. The rest of the evidence would be retained until we received results from the initial examinations, or until other suspects came forward.

I was unable to attend the PM due to other work commitments, but the pathologist described it as one of the worst cases he had ever encountered, noting that several of the wounds could have been fatal. Ultimately the cause of death was determined to be a stab wound to the heart.

Within five days the team at New Scotland Yard identified five individuals based on the fingerprint evidence. Three were the initial suspect who had voluntarily surrendered and the two others she named. By the end of the second week all five suspects were in custody. In interviews they all claimed innocence while pointing the finger at one another, and also all claimed they were unaware of their actions due to the influence of drugs and alcohol.

The jury was having none of it, finding all five guilty of murder. They each received a life sentence.

Chapter 8

Memorable Cases and Mishaps

It was my fourth week as a scene examiner based at Battersea. Mel came in one day, his thick Scottish accent cutting through the quiet. 'Right, Tom, smarten yourself up; we're heading to the house of an important person who's been burgled.' I looked up and quipped, 'We're all important; some just have more money than others.' Mel was unimpressed. 'Just be on your best behaviour and let's do a good job.'

We set off in Mel's police van to an address in an upscale area of Putney. I was struck by the beauty of the Victorian terraced property we approached. It was one of those homes that might serve as a London backdrop in a TV period drama. Carved stone steps led up to a grand oak front door with a large black door-knocker in the centre. With our equipment in hand, we approached the door, and I enjoyed the moment of using the knocker to announce our presence.

A beautifully presented mature woman greeted us with a

warm smile and invited us inside. I didn't recognise her and still had no idea why the couple were supposedly important, but her demeanour was polite and approachable. Mel introduced himself, showcasing the charm he was well known for.

'Good morning! We've been informed that you had an uninvited visitor last night. We're here to see if they left any clues that might help us identify who they were.'

She looked at him, concerned, and replied, 'Yes, I'm quite upset at the thought of someone being in my home while I was asleep.'

'Don't worry; we will do our utmost to find the culprit,' Mel assured her.

As we entered, I took in the elegant décor and antique furniture. The woman explained that the intruder had gained access through a small open window in the ground-floor kitchen at the rear. They appeared to have searched a couple of rooms downstairs and some bedrooms on the first floor. Fortunately, they did not enter the bedroom in which the victim and her husband had been sleeping.

'Tom, why don't you go up and examine the first-floor bedrooms,' said Mel, 'and I'll look around down here.'

Case in hand, I climbed the elegant staircase to the first-floor landing, which had six doors leading off it. Two of the doors were ajar and I decided one of those would be a good starting point for my examination. Entering the room, I saw a large four-poster bed positioned between two expansive windows. The windows were adorned with luxurious curtains, elegantly tied back, with excess fabric flowing over the plush salmon-pink carpet. Antique dressers flanked the bed, and sunlight streamed through the coloured glass of the Tiffany-style bedside lamps, casting beautiful patterns across the room. Scattered throughout the room were several wooden chairs, each with a unique embroidered seat cover, adding a further touch of character.

Wow, I thought to myself. If this is the guest room, what must the master bedroom look like? On the bed lay an open wooden jewellery box, and various items littered the floor, evidence of a burglar in a hurry.

I took out my pot of black carbon-based powder and squirrel hairbrush to examine the light-coloured smooth items. As I was still new in the role, I had filled the pot with powder right to the brim to make sure I didn't run out at a crime scene.

Walking over to the bed with the open pot in hand, I tripped on a rug and the pot went flying through the air. I watched in what seemed like slow motion as a mass of dark powder flew out and began settling on the bed, the furniture and the plush salmon-pink carpet. I glanced in a mirror and saw that I myself was completely coated black. Panic set in. All I could think was that I had to clean the room myself without Mel and the owner discovering what had happened.

The third door I tried off the landing revealed a cleaning cupboard containing a vacuum cleaner, which I grabbed. I plugged it into a socket on the landing and dragged the hose into the bedroom, leaving the wheeled unit just outside the door. As I began vacuuming the carpet, it quickly became apparent that I had made a grave mistake. The powder was so fine that all I was doing was pushing it deeper into the thick carpet fibres, creating unsightly dark tram lines.

To make matters worse, I soon realised that the very fine powder was escaping through the machine's external air vent. I was not only ruining the bedroom but also creating a trail of black powder on the landing.

Meanwhile, down on the ground floor, the homeowner heard the vacuum cleaner running and remarked to Mel, 'Oh, isn't that young chap nice? He's cleaning up after himself.'

Mel, confused, responded, 'Well, that's unusual. He shouldn't be making enough mess to warrant a vacuum cleaner.' Next thing I knew, I heard them both coming upstairs to investigate. I turned off the vacuum and surveyed the damage. It was bad. A wave of dread washed over me and all I could think was — this is it; my career is over. I'd studied nearly five years for nothing.

When they reached the landing, I turned around to face them. A tear rolled down my cheek, making a path through the black powder.

To my surprise, the homeowner was quite forgiving, but Mel was clearly fuming. Back at the station I was instructed to submit a detailed report to the area commander, who was also understandably displeased.

Ultimately, the Met Police agreed to cover half of the damages, and the couple's insurance company covered the rest — apparently the total cost ran into the thousands of pounds. Oh, and the nice woman turned out to be the Lady Mayoress of

London, and her husband was the Lord Mayor. I felt an immense sense of relief that they didn't hold me personally responsible. From that day forward, I was much more careful with my equipment.

Returning from a crime scene, I entered the rear yard of Putney Police Station and found a silver BMW parked in my designated SOCO bay. There was nowhere else for me to park. Seeing the BMW's keys in the ignition, I decided to move the offending vehicle so I could park the SOCO van in its rightful place.

I slid into the driver's seat and started the car. As I glanced at the gear shift, I realised it was automatic rather than the manual shift I was used to. I shifted the car into 'D', whereupon the car began to move slowly forward. Panic set in as I realised there were only two pedals instead of the three I was accustomed to.

In a moment of desperation I pressed down on what I took to be the brake, and to my horror, the car accelerated. For reasons I still can't fathom to this day, I instinctively pressed my foot down even harder on the pedal. The BMW surged forward at speed — straight into the car in front. The impact was so forceful, the BMW climbed onto the other vehicle's hood and I found myself looking directly at the second floor of Putney Police Station.

In complete shock, I kept my foot on the pedal as the back tyres spun wildly on the sealed parking lot, sending plumes of rubber smoke swirling into the air. By now my antics had caught the attention of staff inside the building, who were leaning out of windows to watch the unfolding spectacle. Among them was the owner of the BMW.

I finally snapped out of my shock and took my foot off the accelerator, bringing the wheels to a grinding halt. I opened the door and climbed out onto the hood of the other car before calmly returning to my van, to park it in the recently vacated SOCO bay.

As I walked inside, the station sergeant approached me with a bemused expression. He wanted to be the first to inform me that the car I had just damaged was the inspector's pride and joy. Then he chuckled and shook my hand. 'Well done!' he said. 'Nobody likes him and I guarantee you've made a lot of people in this station happy.'

With that, he turned around and walked back to the front office, laughing all the way. I didn't need to go to the inspector's office; he was already on the warpath and spotted me in the corridor.

'Coyle, get your arse in my office *now*!'

During a severe dressing-down he said I would be responsible for the damage to both vehicles. I stood my ground, referring him to the notice on the wall in the carpark that stated any private vehicles parked there did so at the owner's own risk, and the police held no responsibility for any damage caused.

This only escalated the situation and he threw me out of his office.

The inspector's prized vehicle had to be removed from the

other vehicle by a tow truck equipped with a special lifting device. He submitted an insurance claim, which was denied because the accident had occurred in a private parking lot. The inspector then approached the police union to get them to force me to pay, but they directed him to the signage in the police yard.

The inspector retired not long after, and the story became a bit of a folk tale around the police stations of London.

Most people would quite rightly assume that when a crime examiner shows up to investigate a crime scene, it is safe in the knowledge that the suspect is well gone — either having fled the scene or else in custody. But this is not always the case . . .

Every four weeks we were required to complete a seven-day stint of night duty, focusing exclusively on serious crime scenes across a large section of London. This initiative, introduced in the mid-1990s, aimed to ensure prompt police attendance at incidents involving personal harm. It received strong support from scene examiners, as it allowed us to identify and preserve crucial evidence quickly, rather than waiting until the following morning for the crime scene to be secured.

One significant advantage of this approach was the reduction in interference from frontline uniformed officers, who might inadvertently contaminate evidence through improper handling and packaging. This particularly affected outdoor scenes, where quick action was needed to prevent exposure to the elements and unpredictable weather that could compromise the integrity of the evidence.

One particular night I reported for duty anticipating a quiet shift. Suddenly, uniformed officers were rushing along the corridor in response to an urgent call. I made my way to the call centre, where a communications officer told me someone had been shot and was presumed dead on an estate well known for gang conflicts over drug territory. With nowhere else to be at the time, I stayed in the comms centre to monitor the situation.

It quickly became evident that the victim was not dead but had sustained life-threatening injuries from what appeared to be two gunshot wounds. Paramedics arrived on the scene and began trying to stabilise his condition for transport to Accident & Emergency.

Shortly thereafter, the attending sergeant requested my presence at the crime scene, to search for any clues. Additionally, I was to remain on standby in case they received information about any other premises that could be linked to the shooter and require examination.

Travelling through London at 2 a.m. is a vastly different experience from driving in the daytime. The streets are remarkably quiet — most vehicles on the road at this time of the morning are black cabs, ferrying home the last of the late-night revellers. The only other signs of life are cats sitting on the pavement staring at passing cars, their eyes reflecting the glare of the headlights.

I parked near the police cordon and entered the scene on foot, notebook and pen at the ready. A scene guard was outfitted in full military-style police uniform, complete with helmet. A Heckler & Koch MP5 submachine gun was slung over his shoulder, and he had a Glock 17 9mm self-loading pistol strapped to his waist.

The walkway was flanked by two tower blocks each rising over twenty storeys, and two more blocks of flats stood opposite, part of a vast housing estate. The shooting had taken place in a playground located between the four buildings, designed to provide a recreational space for residents' children. In one corner of the playground there were concrete skateboarding ramps, and another corner featured worn-out swings and a rusty metal slide.

On reaching the inner cordon, I found myself in the centre of a dilapidated basketball court, where the paint was flaking from the sidelines, and the nets were long gone from the hoops. Here I met another officer in military gear, who told me the victim had been taken to hospital. He stressed the need to complete the scene examination before daylight, when residents would begin to emerge from the flats. The paramedics had found bullet entry and exit wounds, and they believed that one of the projectiles might be at the scene.

I went back to my van to gather the necessary equipment, and returned to find three firearms officers on the basketball court in full protective gear, weapons drawn. I thought little of it as I began to collect swabs from the ground, sampling the blood pooling where the victim had fallen. I was taking my third sample when I suddenly heard a firecracker sound in the distance. The surrounding officers immediately raised their weapons, scanning the apartment windows. Concerned, I approached one of the officers and asked if there was a problem.

'Yeah, the shooter is still out there, and they're taking potshots every now and then. We have no idea where they are.'

What? 'You mean I'm out here in the middle of a crime scene with no protective gear, and someone is taking shots at us?'

'Sorry, mate, we thought you were aware of the situation.'

Nope, no one had told me. With that, I packed away my equipment and turned to leave. One of the officers called out, 'Have you finished the scene examination?'

I looked him in the eye and replied, 'Finished? I haven't even started, but there's no way I'm staying here to be shot at.'

I left the scene and went back to the station. The area inspector was waiting for me, clearly having been briefed from the scene. He apologised for the 'miscommunication' regarding the circumstances and requested that I submit an incident report for my senior officers and the police union.

A couple of hours later the suspected shooter was arrested and I was told the area was now secure for examination.

Within a few weeks, all personnel attending active crime scenes were issued with protective vests.

Around the same time, a colleague faced a similarly dangerous situation.

A woman was upstairs in her house and heard strange noises coming from below. Coming downstairs to investigate, she was confronted by an intruder brandishing a knife who attacked her. The woman managed to struggle free, ran out the front door and alerted a neighbour.

The police arrived and searched the property and surrounding area, but found no trace of the suspect. The homeowner was able to give them a description of the intruder, which they broadcast to all nearby units. The woman was then taken to hospital, where her injuries were found to be superficial.

My colleague, who was working nearby, received the call about the incident and went straight to the scene. The responding officers told him the house had been cleared and was ready for examination.

He began his assessment at what was believed to be the point of entry — an open window in the kitchen at the rear of the house. It had all the signs of an opportunistic burglary, as he found fingerprints on the inside of the window consistent with someone climbing in from the outside.

The examiner was working in the living room when he heard a faint noise coming from upstairs. He thought it was probably one of the responding officers but decided to check it out. When he entered one of the bedrooms, the wardrobe door swung open and a knife-wielding man lunged at him. Fortunately, my colleague was no lightweight, standing at 6 foot 4 and built like the proverbial brick shit-house. The intruder just bounced off him, before backing off and bolting down the stairs and out the front door. He was caught a few streets away.

Big and tough he might have been, but my mate was left shaken by the incident. The responding officers expressed their sincere apologies, as it was clear they had not checked the whole house properly. It was a stark reminder of how unpredictable such situations can be, even for seasoned professionals.

Another incident that stands out in my memory involved a case of mistaken identity. Two of my colleagues were working together in central London and both were dispatched to the scene of a robbery at a jewellery store in Hatton Garden. This area was known as 'the diamond district', housing 70 jewellery shops and over 300 jewellery-related businesses.

At the scene they quickly realised the robbery had been a planned, semi-professional operation. CCTV footage showed the two offenders dressed in black, wearing balaclavas and black gloves. It is standard protocol for scene examiners to view recorded footage, which not only shows what happened but, more importantly, allows us to see what the offenders touched with their hands and feet. We always look carefully to see if an offender might have removed their gloves at any point. Trust me, this happens more often than you might think. If they kicked open a door or stood on anything inside the premises, we may be able to develop footwear impressions from those areas. Even seemingly minor details, such as whether any safety glass was broken during the robbery, can be significant. Safety glass shatters into very small pieces, some of which can become embedded in offenders' clothing.

After completing their scene examination, my colleagues left the store and walked along the bustling street back to their van. Suddenly two individuals rushed past them from behind, brandishing a gun and demanding that they hand over their silver crime scene cases. My colleagues quickly complied and the robbers fled around the corner with their stolen goods.

One of the officers issued an urgent request for uniformed backup and it wasn't long before the sound of police sirens filled the air. Within a few minutes the suspects were caught, still in possession of the silver cases they had stolen. The lead investigator took particular satisfaction in revealing to them later that they had actually robbed police officers, and the cases they had stolen contained not wads of cash but equipment designed to catch criminals . . . They were charged with armed robbery and, given their criminal history, told they could expect to spend a significant amount of time 'at Her Majesty's pleasure'.

There are times when the challenges we face extend beyond the obvious villains. One morning I was called to respond to a burglary at a local residence — a large house that had been converted into four flats. Despite having five other cases assigned to me that morning, I decided to prioritise the scene as I was local to the area.

As I approached the house I was greeted by the homeowner, a gracious elderly woman. She welcomed me through the communal front door and, without any prompting, began recounting the details of the incident. She lived in one of the four flats.

I asked the woman which flat had been burgled and she kindly led me to flat three at the top of the stairs. I thanked her for her help and watched her make her way back downstairs. The door to flat three was locked so I knocked, but there was no answer. After 30 seconds of silence I knocked again, a bit louder. Still no response. I knew the victim was in there, as he had told the responding officers he would not leave the flat until I had completed my examination.

After what felt like an eternity, though it was probably only about 40 seconds, I knocked on the door with the full force of my fist. No reply. I began to suspect that the victim had gone out after all, and made my way back downstairs.

'There's no reply, so I presume they've gone out,' I said to the homeowner,

Quick as a flash, she responded, 'No, he's in the flat; I've been out here in the hallway the whole time, and he hasn't come past.'

Now we were both a little concerned.

'I have a key to the flat,' she said. 'I'll let you in, just in case there's a problem.'

We both climbed the stairs and she cautiously opened the flat door with her master key. As I peered inside, I was immediately struck by the intense heat that rushed past me. The heating must have been cranked up to full blast, making the atmosphere quite stifling.

As my eyes adjusted to the darkness, I saw that all the curtains were drawn and there were no lights on inside. I called out the victim's name but received no response. Then I heard groaning noises coming from one of the rooms. I walked cautiously towards the sound and opened a door, to be met with an unexpected sight. A man was lying on the bed, completely naked and pleasuring himself while totally engrossed in a porn film on the TV at the foot of the bed. He was so absorbed in what he was doing that he didn't notice my entrance. At that point I realised his landlady had followed me in and was standing beside me.

I called out the man's name pointedly and he turned his head. Upon seeing the two of us he leapt up, pulled on some clothes and turned off the TV, all within about five seconds. I ushered the landlady out of the room so I could speak to the man alone. Somehow I managed to maintain my professionalism as he showed me around my burglary crime scene.

About 40 minutes later I closed my case and prepared to leave. The victim approached me, extending his hand to shake mine and thanking me for my work. You've got to be kidding, I thought. I knew what that hand had been doing! I politely declined and left.

I found the landlady still waiting in the downstairs hallway. She seemed to be rather amused by the whole situation, remarking that she was having a 'jolly good' time.

I had to wait until I was back in my van before I could have a good laugh myself. This would make a good work story . . .

During a busy shift it was not unusual for a scene examiner to work as many as eight scenes, making the time spent at each location extremely limited. In cases of burglary and vehicle crime, we depended on the reporting officer to help out by walking through the scene with the victim before we got there, to identify which items might be set aside for forensic analysis.

However, in one case I attended, the initial reporting officer must have been asleep during this part of the training at police college.

The crime in question is sometimes known as burglary artifice. This particularly horrible type of crime preys on the most vulnerable members of our community, often the elderly. The criminals gain entry into homes through deceitful means, by posing as representatives from utility services such as water, gas or electricity companies. Once inside, they craftily manipulate their way through the house, often by asking to use the bathroom, while they search for cash and valuables. Their bewildered and defenceless victims stand to lose substantial amounts of cash they may have stashed away, or precious items of sentimental value.

I was halfway through my shift, with four scenes still to examine. I also knew that at any moment my radio might burst to life, summoning me to a serious crime scene. When I knocked, the front door was opened by a pleasant woman who appeared to be around 85 years old. Without hesitation, she invited me inside, not asking for any credentials. I introduced myself before gently advising her to ask for official identification before allowing any stranger into her home in future.

We sat down and she recounted her experience. 'A lovely police officer came yesterday evening,' she said, 'and he looked around my flat.' I could see she was starting to get emotional so I said, 'That's great. Hopefully, I can help find the person who stole your money.'

I asked her to show me the one item I'd been told the police officer had set aside for my examination. She led me into her bedroom, explaining that the officer had placed the item on her bed, so she had slept on the sofa rather than disturb it.

'You didn't need to do that,' I replied, genuinely concerned for her well-being.

She pointed to the object on the bed. 'There it is. I hope you can get something from it.'

I was momentarily speechless. I looked at the item and then back at her. 'Are you sure this is what the officer preserved for me to examine for fingerprints?'

'Oh yes. He picked it up carefully with his pen and put it on the bed.'

The item in question was a pink fluffy slipper.

Apparently the suspect had kicked this slipper across the floor as they completed a search of the bedroom. Yes: a pink fluffy slipper was my one and only supposed source of fingerprints. I was internally fuming at the officer's incompetence, but had to maintain my composure for this poor victim, who had spent the night on the sofa to preserve the integrity of the 'evidence'.

In an effort to reassure her, I opened my case and began to examine the slipper. Then I looked around the flat for any signs of movement or evidence that might have been overlooked. Under the bed I discovered a metal tin. I pulled it out and showed it to the woman, who expressed great delight, telling me it was the tin in which she kept her money, and she had thought the suspect had taken it.

I smiled at her and began to examine the item. To my relief, a clear set of fingerprints began to develop on the surface. The ridge detail indicated that these prints did not belong to the victim, nor could they have come from the officer who had preserved the slipper, as he had clearly not spotted the tin (or much else) during his search.

I documented the prints and later submitted them for analysis. I was relieved when the fingerprint team identified them as belonging to a known offender — a con artist travelling across London, seeking out vulnerable victims. Afterwards, I spoke with the responding officer, who seemed to think the identification had actually originated from the slipper. I shook my head in disbelief. 'Dumb arse,' I muttered to myself, realising the potentially serious implications of his negligence.

To maintain my expert status within the science of fingerprints, I was sometimes seconded to various sections within the police to give me experience of a variety of types of crime. I was assigned for a year to the fraud squad, where I dealt with all sorts of fraudulent crime, on both a national and an international scale. This role required a keen eye for detail, particularly when examining exhibits for friction ridge detail.

About four months in, I was assigned a case involving cheque fraud. For those who don't remember, cheques were paper slips used to authorise payments from an individual's bank account without the need for cash. Before eftpos and online banking became widespread, cheques provided a reliable and reasonably secure way to make payments. But criminals quickly learned that they could steal cheque books from homes and mailboxes, and use them to fraudulently purchase goods. The rise in cheque fraud became a significant issue, resulting in banks losing millions of pounds annually to these white-collar criminals.

Cheques, being made of porous paper, required a specific treatment to develop fingerprints, known as ninhydrin treatment. The chemical ninhydrin reacts with amino acids found in the sweat from our fingers and palms, turning the prints purple.

When we examined a cheque for fingerprints, the placement of the prints provided valuable clues about the suspect. Typically, when a person wrote a cheque, they placed the side of their right or left palm (depending on their handedness) on the paper. This is often referred to as the 'karate chop' or 'writer's palm' position. Then, as the cheque was removed from the cheque book, the suspect inadvertently left their thumbprint on one side, along with the impressions of their fore and middle fingers on the opposite side. This placement provided very helpful information.

While examining a series of cheques from various different cases, I discovered that the developed thumbprint found at the edges of several cheques belonged to the same person, and was consistent with a print from a right hand. I selected the clearest print for analysis and initiated a search against the prints of known fraudsters operating in London at that time. Unfortunately, this search yielded no matches. Next, I turned to AFIS to search against all known offenders in the London region, but again I found no matches. I discussed these findings with my supervisor and we speculated that we might have identified a new fraudster who was not yet in the system.

Over the following weeks, I linked more than 250 cheques to this right thumbprint. It became evident that we were likely dealing with a highly skilled professional fraudster who was adept at evading detection. However, I started to have my doubts when I began to see this same right thumbprint connected to fraud cases right across the UK.

My supervisor and I decided to launch a more in-depth investigation.

I began by visiting the team responsible for collating evidence before it is submitted to the laboratory for chemical treatment. I asked the section supervisor to guide me through the work space to help me better understand their procedures. During my visit, I observed a police officer seated in one corner of the room who was not wearing the mandatory cotton gloves while counting cheques. I watched him occasionally licking his right thumb to assist with handling them.

I returned to my office and reported the incident to my supervisor.

That same day my supervisor requested the officer's fingerprints. By this point we were not greatly surprised that all the thumbprints matched that of the officer. There were also multiple further identifications from his other fingers. Our 'highly skilled professional fraudster' was actually a bumbling police officer. When questioned by his supervisor, the officer claimed ignorance, saying no one had told him he needed to wear gloves when handling exhibits. Within 24 hours he was reassigned to a less demanding position.

One of the most complicated fingerprint identification cases I was a part of during my career involved identifying a group of people killed in a small plane crash, out in the countryside. Upon impact, the plane caught fire, resulting in the deaths of everyone on board.

The aircraft was on a parachuting flight, carrying a set of skydiving instructors and then those who were preparing to accompany them on tandem dives. The people on board were a mix of tourists and locals, resulting in a higher level of media coverage than usual.

A police DVI search and rescue team was dispatched to the crash site along with members of the Air Accident Investigation Unit to recover and preserve the remains of the deceased and investigate the cause of the crash. After the recovery process, the bodies were flown to the department of forensic pathology for examination.

I was asked to attend with a team to assist with the DVI mortuary phase, primarily focused on identifying the victims through fingerprints. Since this was a closed disaster, we knew the names of those on board; however, due to the severe injuries inflicted by the fire, visual identification was not feasible. Before heading to the mortuary we were told that it might be impossible to obtain finger or palm prints because of the burn injuries. How many times had we heard that before?

The team consisted of two forensic pathologists, a police photographer, two exhibits officers, an inspector designated as the DVI team lead, three police forensic fingerprint specialists, and myself. Before we entered the changing area we were told that the bodies were already in the mortuary, and that we might be in for a surprise when we first saw them. I noticed a mix of intrigue and anticipation on several faces in the room. Everyone was eager to get started.

In the changing room the distinctive smell of burnt bodies permeated the air. Burnt bodies emit a unique odour different from that of decomposing remains. Put simply, they smell like overcooked pork, particularly the crackling, which can give off a strong burnt scent. I must admit that after examining bodies exposed to fire, I often find myself avoiding roast pork for a few weeks.

In full PPE we proceeded to the mortuary, where it soon became clear why we had been prepared beforehand. On one examination table lay a single body, severely burned over every part of its surface. The other tables each held two bodies, on their bottoms with their legs flat and forward, one behind the other. From their arrangement, it was clear that they had been joined together for a tandem parachute jump. Despite having examined hundreds of dead bodies in my career, I had never seen anything like this. At this point I realised that we would be here for the full day — this would be a particularly challenging investigation.

We focused first on the body on its own, likely to be that of the pilot. The photographer documented the body in situ before the exhibits officers removed the severely burned clothing and jewellery, cataloguing each item on a DVI form.

Removing clothing from a badly burnt body is a delicate process because of how the heat affects different fibres. Plant-based fibres such as cotton, bamboo and linen tend to ignite quickly, leaving behind ashy remnants. Synthetic fibres such as polyester and nylon, in contrast, often melt in high temperatures, resulting in a shiny, plastic-like residue that sticks to the skin. This melted material can be particularly hard to remove without taking away the epidermal layer of skin along with it.

With the burnt clothing removed, the body was rephotographed, and then my colleague and I took over. The body was charred and blackened, with around 70 per cent of the skin severely damaged and hardened from the intense heat of the fire. There are four levels of burn that a victim can receive in a serious fire. First-degree burns only affect the outer layer of the skin, the epidermis, causing redness. Second-degree burns damage the epidermal and dermal skin layers, and will also cause blistering and swelling. Third-degree burns destroy the epidermal and dermal skin layers, as well as damaging muscles, nerves and deeper fat tissues. The affected areas appear leathery or charred.

These bodies all displayed signs of fourth-degree burns, where the damage extends to tendons and bones.

I started by examining one of the hands. The skin was noticeably raised, extremely hard, and felt brittle. The fingers had curled into a fist from tissue shrinkage and muscle contraction. Interestingly, this clenching sometimes serves to preserve the fingerprint details, so we had to open the fingers. But as soon as I tried to gently open the cold, damp hand, the skin on the back started to flake and crumble. Eventually I decided the best way to unclench the fingers would be to use a post-mortem print spoon.

I gently placed the metal device over the tip of the victim's forefinger, while keeping the rest of the hand firmly anchored against the table. As I applied pressure, the finger began to straighten, though a little more charred skin flaked off from the back of the hand. Unfortunately, I soon heard the dreaded 'snap' — the sound of a finger joint or bone breaking under the pressure of the mortuary spoon. However, once it was finally straightened, I was able to assess the damage to the charred epidermal layer. Under magnification, it was obvious there was minimal ridge detail visible.

With the pathologist's permission, I carefully removed the charred skin from the finger. On the inner surface of this skin, I was able to detect detailed ridge formation, including a pattern. I placed the charred skin on a towel and used a specialised lens and digital camera to capture the details on the inside curved surface.

In such cases, we also use a special forensic putty called Mikrosil to preserve details in a three-dimensional format. This compound sets quickly and provides excellent microscopic detail. However, once it is mixed with the hardener, you have only about 30 seconds to apply it before it becomes unusable.

Using a plastic surgical spatula, I applied the mixed Mikrosil compound to the inner surface of the charred skin, ensuring the putty covered the entire area. In just a couple of minutes the Mikrosil had set to a rubber-like consistency. I then gently removed the charred skin from the putty, revealing a perfect fingerprint. We repeated this process for all fingers and thumbs, as we didn't know which prints we would have for comparison from the collection of the AM data.

Next, we turned our attention to the victim's feet. Typically, individuals are wearing some type of footwear, which helps safeguard the feet from severe heat damage. In this case the victim had been wearing boots, so his soles were only partially burnt. These prints could be easily documented using black powder and large sticky white labels.

At this stage we prepared to examine the skydiving instructors, who were still connected to their tandem partners. Looking closely, we could see that they were attached by their parachuting harnesses. However, the material of the harnesses and their clothing had melted together, creating a glue-like bond between the two bodies in each pair.

Carefully, and with a bit of strength, the pathologist pulled them apart, and we examined them in the same manner as we had the first body. We split into teams, each examining one pair of bodies.

Several of the victims had severely burnt feet because they had been wearing thin trainers, which didn't provide the same level of protection as boots. In these cases we had to peel away the burnt epidermal layer from the soles in order to photograph and cast the inner surface using Mikrosil. In the process, we had to handle the charred skin with great care to prevent it from crumbling or breaking, leaving us with nothing to examine. It was very time-consuming, but there was no alternative.

Over the next few days we began receiving AM data for the locals involved in the plane crash — the pilot and the set of parachute instructors. Gathering AM data for the overseas victims took a little longer. Once we had all the AM data, we could compare the detail developed from personal items to the ridge detail recorded from the PM. All the victims were identified within a few days, and the coroner authorised the release of the bodies to their families.

Many forensic examiners dread attending court to provide expert evidence. The environment is intimidating, and while we are all well versed in our areas of expertise, some lawyers have a knack of leading witnesses astray. They may divert the discussion away from the evidence at hand, prompting responses that stray far from the original material under discussion. This is why, early in our careers, we are advised to take a moment to process a question before replying. Consider your response carefully and, where possible, stick to simple 'yes' or 'no' answers. If elaboration is required, aim for clarity and concision.

I was called to provide expert forensic evidence at a murder trial at the Central Criminal Court of England and Wales, known as the Old Bailey. This court has a formidable reputation, adding to the anxiety witnesses naturally feel when summoned to give evidence.

The first recorded mention of the Old Bailey was in 1585, since when it has undergone several reconstructions at various locations in London. The current building, completed in 1902, is on a street named Old Bailey. Since its establishment, the court has held more than 250,000 trials, resulting in 475 sentences of death and execution. The court complex consists of eighteen courtrooms spread across three levels, along with 70 holding cells for prisoners in the basement.

I was due to give evidence in courtroom one, which has hosted some of the most sensational criminal trials in British history, including that of Dr Crippen, who was hanged in 1910 for poisoning and dismembering his wife; serial killer Peter Sutcliffe, known as the Yorkshire ripper, who murdered thirteen women and attempted to kill seven others in the late 1970s; and English gangsters the Kray twins.

Upon entering the courtroom you are immediately enveloped by a sense of history. The first thing that captures your attention is the striking glass ceiling, surrounded by intricately designed hand-carved plaster coving, which adds an air of grandeur to the room. Central to the courtroom is a raised gallery, elegantly crafted from oak, where the defendant is seated during the trial. On one side of the courtroom, tiered seating accommodates the prosecution and defence lawyers, known as King's Counsel, or KCs. These are senior legal practitioners appointed by the Crown in recognition of their exceptional skill and expertise in advocacy.

Across the other side sit the twelve jury members, with strategically placed screens that allow them to closely examine evidence presented during the trial. In the centre of the room a large table is reserved for court registrars and other staff facilitating the administrative aspects of the proceedings.

Balcony seating on either side of the room accommodates about 100 members of the public, and at the far end of the courtroom is a raised platform that seats the presiding judge. It is a grand old venue.

As usual, I set off for court in good time to navigate the usual heavy traffic and any potential delays. This meant I arrived at court early, and there's nothing worse than pacing the corridors of a courthouse, anticipating the moment you must give evidence to a roomful of strangers. The wait can be excruciating.

I found myself going over and over my evidence, trying to suppress thoughts of the challenging questions that counsel might pose. I watched other witnesses being called in, their expressions serious, and noted the obvious relief on their faces when they came out.

Finally it was my turn. The court usher opened the door and announced in a deep monotone, 'The court requests Mr Coyle.' I stepped forward, my paperwork securely held in a black folder, and made my way to the witness box.

I was there to provide forensic evidence in a high-profile murder case involving a Jamaican gang known as The Yardies. Two of their members were accused of murdering two people in an apparent revenge attack. My testimony focused on fingerprints developed from several key exhibits, which had been linked to both defendants.

The accused clearly had some supporters in the public gallery. During my testimony they began clicking their tongues and making a sound by sucking air through their teeth, which felt intimidating. From previous experience, I knew they were warning me. Eventually the judge ordered them to stop. As I identified the two defendants in relation to the fingerprints on the exhibits, the disruptive noise escalated; there were about eight of them now. Observing that their antics were having the desired effect of ruining my concentration, the judge ordered security to remove them. As they were ushered out they shouted threats at me, saying they would be waiting.

I continued my testimony without further interference. After being questioned by the prosecutor and cross-examined by the defence, my testimony concluded after about two hours.

As I left the courtroom, I wore the same relieved smile as I had observed on the faces of previous witnesses. But when I stepped out onto the street I spotted the noisy bunch who had been ejected. They were staring directly at me. I picked up my pace heading away from court but they began to follow. I could hear them getting closer, their taunts growing louder, with one of them shouting, 'You're a dead man!' Shit. Panic started to set in.

Just then a police car pulled up and the driver shouted, 'Get in!' I didn't need asking twice. I dived into the back seat and we pulled away from the kerb.

The officer driving turned to me and said, 'That was a close call. I don't like to think what would have happened if they'd caught you.' He explained that he had been in the courtroom and seen the men removed. Anticipating trouble, he'd waited in his vehicle for me to emerge from the court. His quick thinking saved me, and I felt overwhelming relief and gratitude.

Chapter 9

Moving to New Zealand

I had been employed by the London Metropolitan Police for over fifteen years and had achieved the rank of senior forensic practitioner. In this role I managed several scene examiners and oversaw serious crime scenes. However, as changes unfolded within the police, I found myself increasingly disillusioned. Budget constraints meant they were reverting back to the system of three separate forensic positions — fingerprint officer, SOCO and scene scientist — as the cost of training people to cover all three roles was said to be too high.

I had been posted to many different stations around London, and seconded back to New Scotland Yard on several occasions to work on specialist teams. As well as the fraud squad, I had spent six months on the anti-terrorism team, where my role included examining critical evidence related to bomb-making equipment and locations tied to terrorist activities both in the UK and abroad.

I was grateful for these diverse experiences, but I felt that my true expertise lay in the field of crime scene examination. I had developed a keen intuition for understanding where suspects had been within crime scenes; I think of this as my 'sixth sense'. It allows me to not only identify where they may have been but also the specific items they likely interacted with.

Allie and I both needed a break, so we booked a three-week holiday to New Zealand with our daughter Hannah, and visited Allie's sister and family, who had settled there ten years earlier. After we had recovered from the exhausting 36-hour journey and resulting jet lag, we were finally able to experience the true beauty of the country we had heard so much about.

A saying I had heard from UK travellers to New Zealand rang true: 'You switch your clocks forward twelve hours, but the lifestyle is twenty years behind.' I instantly fell in love with New Zealand, and understood that all the hype we had heard from Allie's sister was true. In 2003 New Zealand truly was a green and clean country, characterised by unspoiled landscapes and endless shorelines. This was a stark contrast to Benidorm and Tenerife, two of the popular destinations for UK holidaymakers.

In New Zealand, charming wooden villas lined the streets, each different from its neighbours, in contrast to the mainly uniform brick terraced houses back home. While times and landscapes inevitably change, my affection for New Zealand today remains unwavering.

During that trip we stayed with Allie's sister Karen and her husband Mark. Karen is warm-hearted and somewhat shy, while Mark is the complete opposite: free-spirited and sociable, with a penchant for a drink or two. They both took time off work to be our private guides and show us the sights New Zealand had to offer. I remember vividly our visit to Russell in the Bay of Islands, where I sat alone on a hill watching the endless views across the bays and deciding there and then that moving here was the change we needed — if it was at all possible.

Partway through our trip I received an email from a former Met colleague who was now working as a forensic fingerprint officer with the New Zealand Police. He suggested we meet up in Auckland, and kindly offered me a tour of the forensic section at Auckland Central Police Station. I showed up in shorts and T-shirt, looking every bit the tourist (but minus the camera slung around my neck).

My former colleague had changed significantly since our London days. He had a more relaxed demeanour and wore casual clothing, with long hair tied back and a beard. I was eager to hear about his work, so he led me to the seventh floor, where we entered an open-plan office that resembled the fingerprint offices at New Scotland Yard in the early 1990s. He introduced me to each of the twelve staff members, all of whom seemed genuinely pleased to meet me and made me feel right at home.

Each officer had their own desk and monitor, and they were all busy sorting through various pieces of evidence that were spread across their work spaces. The other half of the seventh floor was dedicated to the forensic laboratory, which housed all the equipment needed to develop fingerprints from various substrates.

While it wasn't the tidiest of workplaces, stepping into the lab filled me with excitement. The sights and smells ignited a sense of enthusiasm within me, and I knew it was a place in which I could thrive.

I met the section supervisor, who held the rank of senior sergeant, equivalent to the rank of inspector in the Met. He greeted me with a warm smile and asked, 'How do you like our little setup, then?'

'From what I've seen, it looks really good,' I replied.

'Well, we have an opening for a forensic fingerprint officer if you're interested . . .' he added quickly.

I sat there for a few seconds in a daze before replying. 'Oh! Well, I wasn't expecting to hear that!'

'If you're interested, you can come back in a couple of days to complete some tests and have an interview, and we'll see where we go from there.'

The rest of the tour felt like a blur. My mind was consumed with the news that I could, if I wanted, be interviewed for a job in New Zealand in just a few days.

All the way back to Karen and Mark's, my mind was whirring with the implications. Tempted though I was, I felt confused and bewildered by the thought of uprooting our lives in England. I talked it over with Allie, who said she would support whatever I wanted to do. I sensed that, deep down, she also craved some change away from London. If we were going to make such a move, we thought, the time was now, with Hannah young enough to transition well.

Two days later I found myself heading back to the police station for my interview, this time dressed a bit more formally. Based on my previous interviews, I was expecting a formal 'yes sir, no sir' atmosphere, but to my relief the interviewers made me feel at ease and relaxed.

After various practical tests related to fingerprints and forensic crime scene examination, I was taken into the supervisor's office, where an HR representative was also waiting. We spent about an hour chatting about my previous experience and my work with processing exhibits in the laboratory. I was then asked to step out of the office while they discussed whether I would be a good fit for the team.

After about five minutes I was called back in. The supervisor extended his hand and shook mine, saying, 'The job's yours if you want it.' He smiled. 'Take some time to talk it over with your family and discuss it with your current employers. We'll keep the position open for you for four weeks.'

Upon returning to the UK, I promptly met with my supervising officer to discuss my job offer. He presented the opportunity to the relevant decision-makers, and within a few days I was told that if I chose to accept the role in New Zealand, my position within the Metropolitan Police would remain open for six months. This meant that if it didn't work out, I could return to my current role.

The decision at that point became very straightforward.

I had nothing to lose.

In the space of five months (May to October 2003) I went through a series of major transitions: I was offered a new job on the other side of the world; I resigned from my position at the Metropolitan Police; we sold our house; and we arranged for all our belongings to be shipped in a container to New Zealand.

Our departure was emotional — many tears were shed at the airport as Allie and Hannah and I said goodbye to parents and grandparents and siblings. No longer would visiting them be a matter of a two-hour drive from London. Had we made the right decision? It felt huge.

One of the first things I noticed in my first days in New Zealand was the different pace of life. It all felt so much more relaxed on the streets after the mad frenzy of London. Here, there was plenty of space to walk freely without the need to navigate around others. I was also captivated by the sight of some children going to school without shoes or socks, joyfully bouncing around as if they were heading to the beach. That would never happen in the UK because of the danger of glass fragments on the street.

Even the way news was presented was different. In New Zealand, the national news included coverage of crimes in regional areas, whereas in the UK only the most serious crimes outside London, such as a multiple murder, would typically make national headlines.

While I adapted to most changes relatively quickly, there was one adjustment that still confuses me twenty years later: how can you have Christmas in the summer? For nearly four decades, Christmas for me was synonymous with cold winter days and long, dark nights. By six o'clock on a winter evening, most people would be indoors watching television. If they went out during the day at all it was bundled up in layers of thick woollen clothing.

In New Zealand at Christmas people headed out into the warm weather, relaxing in their garden or picnicking at one of the numerous beaches. Christmas Day was especially surreal. I was accustomed to huddling around a fake fire, eating overcooked turkey with all the trimmings. I am still adjusting to the idea of celebrating in shorts and T-shirts, grilling sausages on the barbecue while enjoying a steady flow of beer or wine.

On my first day at work I was assigned a desk, completed all the initiation paperwork, then met the office supervisor. It was only then that I learned I had officially been employed as a forensic fingerprint officer, not a forensic practitioner. My employment contract stipulated that my focus would be solely on the science of fingerprints, within the office or at serious crime scenes, allowing me to assist with other forensic procedures only if absolutely necessary.

The New Zealand Police still had distinct differentiation between the roles of staff who attended serious crime scenes. For all crimes up to and including armed robbery, a SOCO would respond. In cases involving suspicious death, murder or an act of terrorism, specialists — often forensic fingerprint officers and other experts from the Environmental Science and Research centre (ESR) — would be called in as well. ESR (today known as the Institute for Public Health and Forensic Science) was a quasi-governmental agency whose role was to gather forensic evidence at serious crime scenes.

My team in Auckland was primarily responsible for processing fingerprints from crime scenes located throughout a substantial area of the North Island. But as the largest fingerprint section in the country, we got to attend some serious crime scenes to collaborate with staff from ESR. Ours was the only fingerprint section in New Zealand that had a dedicated fingerprint officer on standby 24/7, 365 days a year, including Christmas Day. Each officer was assigned to this standby seven-day shift at least every eight weeks. So I would get some crime scene work.

Additionally, I was pleased to discover that the Department of Forensic Pathology in Auckland, commonly referred to as the forensic mortuary, was the busiest in the country. It managed all cases involving unidentified deceased, suspicious deaths and homicides throughout the North Island. As part of my role, I was tasked with attending these cases to document finger and palm prints for identification purposes, and to assist in the collection of forensic evidence during post-mortems.

After three weeks in the office I was keen to get out into the field and engage directly with crime scenes. One morning a colleague asked for my assistance at a murder scene and I eagerly agreed. We arrived at the cordon and were greeted by the mandatory scene guard, along with the officer in charge from the Criminal Investigation Branch (CIB). Two civilian examiners from ESR were also present, tasked with collecting forensic evidence other than fingerprints.

As a new officer, I stepped aside while my colleague talked to the others present. I desperately wanted to take the lead and conduct the entire examination myself, but I knew this was not the day for that. During the examination I noticed that the ESR staff, while undoubtedly competent, lacked the appropriate forensic equipment. For example, they had to rely on a SOCO to apply basic black powder to the floor in order to obtain footwear impressions. It was frustrating to see five people at work at the crime scene, all trying to gather and preserve forensic evidence, and I couldn't help but feel annoyed by the inefficiency.

Back at the office I expressed my frustration to my supervisors, saying I could easily have conducted the whole examination by myself. They reminded me that I had been employed as a forensic fingerprint officer.

During the first few months I assisted at various serious crime scenes, and I often found myself frustrated with the procedures for locating, developing and preserving evidence. It wasn't until six months later that I was finally added to the on-call roster and given the opportunity to attend serious crime scenes on my own. From this point I began to build relationships with the staff at ESR, who were aware of my background in the UK. They welcomed me with open arms and allowed me to assist them to locate other forensic evidence in addition to fingerprints. Before long, I was involved in a range of forensic work, from developing footwear impressions and DNA sampling to more complex procedures such as the application of luminol, a chemical reagent used to detect blood.

My bosses were not particularly happy that I was recovering other forensic evidence in addition to fingerprints. They kept reminding me of my role, but I insisted that if my assistance was needed by ESR and I could collect evidence without disrupting the scene or involving others unnecessarily, there should be no issue. After I was promoted to senior fingerprint officer, my supervisor relented somewhat. I continued collaborating with ESR staff as much as possible. I was committed to obtaining the best forensic evidence to support ongoing investigations, and I took every opportunity to contribute effectively to the process.

Strange as it may sound, one role in which I truly thrived, aside from examining crime scenes, was examining cadavers. Over the years I began visiting the mortuary regularly, to the point where I was on a first-name basis with all the staff. I often found myself sitting down with them to enjoy a coffee and discuss various cases.

During one of my mortuary visits I was told that a person had been struck by a train and was in several pieces on the examination table. I was advised not to lift the white sheet because the injuries were particularly severe.

I needed to obtain records of the victim's fingers and palms, so I cautiously lifted the sheet to locate a hand. The body was indeed in several pieces, to the extent that the fingers were almost severed from the palm, with only tendons holding them in place. It took me some time to identify which finger was which before I could accurately record them. Somehow, I managed to produce a full record of the fingers and palm from both hands so I could try to identify the victim back at the police station.

On another occasion, before I examined the deceased, the pathologist warned me that the body was so badly burnt that identification through fingerprints would be impossible. The body had been recovered from a car fire that left no identifiable features on the face or most of the body.

As I entered the mortuary, the distinctive stench of charred flesh filled the air. I found that the hands of the deceased were tightly clenched from the intense heat of the fire. As I tried to prise the fingers away from the palm, chunks of skin began to fall away, revealing the extent of the damage. After about twenty minutes of careful work I had opened all the fingers on both hands, but in the process, I had managed to break some of them.

I knew the standard procedure of ink and paper for fingerprinting was not feasible on this occasion. Instead, I employed a technique known as casting, which I detail in

Chapter 8. This allowed me to capture ridge detail from several fingers and the palm. Back in my office, I searched the detail against our database, successfully identifying the deceased individual. When I returned to the mortuary a few days later, the pathologist acknowledged my skills with a nod of respect, stating that he would never again question my abilities!

I was asked to assist with the post-mortem of a female murder victim. It was alleged that she had been strangled and beaten by her partner. After the forensic pathologist completed the initial PM, I was tasked with examining the victim to highlight any bruising, especially around the wrists and neck.

In order to conduct this examination, I needed to move the body into a completely dark room in order to use an alternate light source (ALS) machine. This high-intensity device uses twelve separate light wavebands, ranging from white light at 000 nanometres to red light at 650 nanometres. This enhances the visibility of physical trace evidence that is typically invisible to the naked eye.

Unfortunately the only available space was a small storage room, which barely accommodated the deceased on a trolley along with me. I set up the ALS and also positioned my digital camera on a tripod, equipped with specialised filters, to capture any findings. Then I turned off the lights, plunging the room into complete darkness. Just me and a cadaver in a darkened cupboard . . .

I activated the light source and began to examine the body for bruising using a frequency of 350 nanometres, known as ultraviolet (UV) light. Invisible to the human eye, this frequency has earned the nickname 'black light'. When it shines on certain materials, they absorb the UV light and re-emit it as visible light. Beginning at the base of the feet and working my ways towards the head, I recorded with my specialised camera any areas that reacted to the light. I observed a reaction around the victim's wrists and neck.

As I lifted the light source wand slightly, I was startled to see the victim's wide-open eyes glowing under the light, staring straight back at me. It was quite a shock and I had to take a moment to regain my composure in that dark little room. I continued the examination, utilising all twelve light frequencies, and from time to time reminding my brain about the eyes so I wouldn't take fright when I saw them again. The images I captured showed pressure points on the body that corroborated the pathologist's conclusion that the suspect had forcefully held the victim and strangled her.

Throughout my career, I have examined dead bodies at every stage of decomposition, from those who have recently passed away to those who have been deceased for weeks or even months. People often ask whether I am affected by what I see, but to be honest, the only instances that have affected me deeply involved the examination of children or elderly who have been victims of violence.

I have been present at post-mortems of children as young as three months old. As a parent myself, I have found it impossible not to feel a sense of sorrow and even anger in these situations.

However, I have learned to activate an invisible switch in my mind that allows me to compartmentalise those emotions and focus on my professional responsibilities. It would be inappropriate for me to describe such cases in detail.

It is essential also for someone in my position to respect a deceased person's religious beliefs and cultural practices. I once attended a Māori tangihanga (funeral) where fingerprints were needed from the victim. Upon arriving at the victim's home, I found the whānau pani (bereaved family) gathered together. In Māori culture it is believed that the spirit of the tūpāpaku (deceased) lingers around the body for a few days after death. I was greeted by a person who guided me into a room where family members sat around an open casket, sharing stories and memories (waikōrero) about the deceased.

I took a moment to sit with the family and explain my intentions to them and to the tūpāpaku. Then, with the assistance of a family member, I recorded prints from all eight fingers and both thumbs. After cleaning the hands afterwards, I apologised to the whānau and tūpāpaku for interrupting their tuku (farewell) and left. This remains one of the most sombre moments of my career.

After nine years' service in New Zealand and undergoing additional training, I was appointed forensic laboratory manager for the police in Auckland. The laboratory processed thousands of exhibits annually, from throughout the North Island, collected by both police and Customs. One of my first jobs was to modernise the laboratory and enhance its ability to manage the increasing workload. I initiated a comprehensive overhaul of the lab's infrastructure, focusing on modernising equipment and improving workflow.

One of the changes was the introduction of new LCN standards and refined work practices, to enable us to extract DNA from even minute samples. We also acquired specialised cabinets for the safe storage of the various chemicals used in fingerprint development. This enhanced our ability to handle different substrates in compliance with safety standards. The photographic room was updated to facilitate the use of ALS equipment, allowing staff to capture high-quality images of evidence in controlled environments, including pitch-black settings.

In my new role I collaborated with Customs officers, mostly in relation to their seizures of imported illegal drugs. Drug smugglers went to great lengths to disguise the transport of narcotics through both air freight and postal services. I saw numerous extraordinarily creative techniques used by smugglers to conceal drugs within everyday items or even integrate them directly into materials such as candles or drinks. Drugs have been found hidden in statues, pencils, electronic devices, power tools, furniture and steel pipes, among many other items. One day a team of Customs officers visited our forensic lab to deliver thousands of yellow rubber ducks, each one stuffed with pseudoephedrine, a precursor for the synthesis of methamphetamine, or 'P'.

I was once invited to participate in a Customs raid on a South Auckland warehouse suspected of being a hub for drug traffickers. After an early-morning briefing at their offices, about fifteen Customs officers and I travelled in three vans to a location a few streets away from the warehouse. We settled in to wait — and wait, reminding me how tedious such operations could be. I remembered why I had not offered to participate in many raids in London. Eventually we received the call to 'GO, GO, GO!' — and we did.

I maintained a safe distance as the Customs officers conducted their search, resulting in the arrest of three suspects. In New Zealand, Customs officers have the authority to arrest individuals under the Customs and Excise Act 2018.

I entered the sizeable warehouse once the suspects were secured, and walked around the unit with the lead Customs officer. The warehouse spanned two levels, and the ground floor was an open-plan storage area, equipped with a couple of forklifts. In one corner several wooden crates were neatly stacked and encased in plastic wrapping. The officers suspected these boxes contained drugs.

While they examined the crates, I climbed to the first floor to some offices, in which I found various documents. Later inspection showed these to contain handwritten notes detailing times, amounts and locations of drugs concealed within imported items.

I began the process of examining the three offices, applying white and black powder to fingerprint items that were likely to yield usable prints. I collected the paperwork for laboratory analysis using the chemical ninhydrin to develop the fingerprints. Within two hours I lifted around 25 fingerprints, gathered 60–70 pieces of paper, and collected eight DNA swabs from various drink bottles.

When I returned to the ground floor I was told that the crates had indeed contained signs of drugs. A special Customs van was ordered to transport the crates to their base for examination. I accompanied them to verify that the seized items were properly handled. By the end of the day I had another fifteen fingerprint lifts from the items inside the boxes. I also transported 60 flat-packed boxes to be treated with ninhydrin.

By the end of the week I had 40 fingerprint lifts from the scene itself and a further 35 clear images of fingers and palms from the boxes and paperwork. I searched the most promising prints against the database and identified seven individuals, four of whom proved crucial to the investigation.

It was a pivotal and fulfilling stage in my career. As a forensic laboratory manager I also had the opportunity to teach forensic techniques to both sworn and non-sworn recruits. My role still involved regular visits to the mortuary, attending serious crime scenes, and identifying individuals through fingerprints, palm prints and footprints.

There is nothing more rewarding than arriving at a crime scene or mortuary where there are no leads or suspects, and going on to locate, develop and preserve prints that turn out to be crucial. The process of uncovering a match in the database is exhilarating. Then it is a matter of preparing and presenting evidence in court, based on our findings. We talk about this as a 'cradle to grave' service, as we are involved from the initial investigation through to the courtroom. This combination of such a variety of fulfilling roles brought me a deep sense of satisfaction.

At this time, those of us working in the forensic science division of the New Zealand Police did not participate in disaster victim identification (DVI) training, as senior management did not deem it necessary. This changed in March 2008, when I became the first forensic fingerprint officer to attend a DVI course at the National Police Training Centre in Porirua, Wellington. The two-week training was intense and covered every aspect of disaster victim identification.

At the end of it, I was proud to be recognised as an official member of the DVI team. I didn't know it at the time, but this would signal a new direction for my work.

Chapter 10

Every Contact Leaves a Trace

I was midway through a week of on-call duties, during which I was on standby for serious crime scenes requiring specialist examination. It was 3 p.m. and I was finalising a statement for an upcoming court case when I received a call from a detective stationed in New Zealand's Far North district. There had been a murder and he requested my presence to examine the scene. At that stage they had no leads.

The location was about a five-hour drive from Auckland, so I knew I needed to prepare for an extended stay. I notified my supervisor, then I packed the van with everything I would need. I didn't want to run out of anything when I was five hours' drive from my base. It's not as if I could pop to the local dairy for fingerprint powder.

I nipped home to collect a change of clothes, some extra police overalls, an overnight bag and a bag of lollies for the long drive. Then I set off. Arriving at the district police station around

9 p.m., I headed to the briefing room, where the lead investigator told me the scene had been secured and was being monitored overnight by scene guards. They were expecting to see me and the photographer first thing in the morning.

I checked in to the hotel where I and some other officers from Auckland would be staying. When small rural towns face a murder investigation, officers from the nearest major city often assist local investigators.

The next morning, after an early briefing, I headed to the crime scene with the exhibits officer, the photographer and an ESR representative.

'The body is in the living room, seated in a chair,' a detective at the scene told us. 'It looks like he was eating dinner at the time. Initial reports suggest he was killed with a firearm, likely a shotgun.' After a short pause he went on. 'It's quite messy, as the wounds are to the head, so be careful of any remains surrounding the body.'

Given that experienced detectives often underplay the grisly detail, this was a warning to be heeded.

The house was a small single-storey villa surrounded by several outbuildings. The exhibits officer took the lead, placing metallic stepping plates around the house to protect areas of the floor that might contain crucial evidence such as blood trails, hair, fibres or footwear impressions. The photographer then entered to document the entire scene before the ESR officer and I began our examination, as our work would inevitably alter the scene. After about 40 minutes we received the all-clear to enter.

I approached the front door and carefully stepped onto the first stepping plate.

Navigating these plates can be challenging. They each measure only about 40 cm by 30 cm, making it tricky to step from one to another without falling in the very area we're trying to protect. Also, there is a limited number of plates, so we often had to move and reposition them to examine other areas. Scene examiners often examine the floor first, so the plates can then be removed.

As I inspected the front door and its surrounding frame, I looked for any signs of damage that might indicate a forced entry. I found none. I then inspected the rear door and windows, coming to the same conclusion.

In the living room, the deceased was seated in an armchair in the centre of the room, facing a television that was still on, broadcasting one of those cheerful morning shows. On his lap rested a plate with the remnants of his dinner. I can vividly recall the details: beef, potatoes, carrots and peas, all generously covered with gravy.

His hands, resting on the chair armrests, were still grasping his knife and fork, as if he was poised to enjoy his evening meal. While the body appeared largely untouched, the head was another matter. The lower portion of the jaw and the sides of the cheeks remained, but the rest of the head was gone. The suspect had likely approached from behind and fired a shotgun or similar at the back of his head. Death would have been instant. He wouldn't even have known it was coming.

I continued my walkthrough and determined that the main areas for investigation were the living room and the back door. There was nothing in any of the other rooms that suggested an intruder had entered. Given that there were no signs of a struggle in the living room, or any significant items of interest on the carpet, we decided it was safe to remove the plates from this area, allowing us to examine the scene more easily.

By this time it was around 11 a.m. It being midsummer, the temperature was beginning to rise, as was the odour from the body. Flies had started to gather around the open wounds on his head. We needed to examine the body first so we could send it to Auckland as soon as possible for post-mortem.

As I examined the area around the dead man, I felt something land on my shoulder. Thinking it was a fly, I ignored it. A few minutes later I felt something on my other shoulder. I finally looked up and realised what was happening. Parts of the man's brain and skull had stuck to the ceiling and were now drying in the heat and becoming unstuck. Just another grim reminder of what our job can involve.

We finished our examination of the body and the surrounding area and it was time to have the victim transported to Auckland. Because rigor mortis had set in, there were some logistical considerations. Rigor mortis is a natural process that occurs after death, typically setting in within an hour or two. It involves a temporary stiffening of the muscles caused by a buildup of calcium in the muscle tissue. Rigor mortis begins in the face and neck and progresses throughout the body, reaching its peak within twelve hours, before gradually loosening over the next twelve hours. Moving a body in full rigor mortis requires considerable force that can damage the body, so it is best to allow the body to complete this stage, approximately 24 hours after death, before trying to move it.

We were confident that this body had been in position for at least 21 hours, meaning rigor mortis had almost completed its course and the muscles were relaxing. We laid out a body bag, and three of us carefully lifted the deceased onto the bag, ensuring we did not cause further damage or disrupt any forensic evidence such as gunshot residue or potential hairs and fibres. Deceased bodies can be unexpectedly heavy and difficult to move around.

We found very little else of evidential value inside the property. It appeared that the suspect had entered through the unlocked back door, walked directly to the living room, shot the victim, and left the way they came in. The only other areas that required full forensic examination were the area outside the back door and the door itself.

The evidence we recovered included footwear impressions from indentations in the soil at the back of the house, fingerprints on various areas of the rear door and its frame, gunshot residue from the rear of the chair, and some fibre and hair from the chair and the floor leading to it from the rear door. ESR documented the direction of the discharged firearm and collected samples of the shot that had penetrated the opposite wall.

We returned to the station, where we found the case had

progressed rapidly over the past few hours. The lead investigator was on the phone to a suspect, trying to calm him and persuade him to surrender. After a few hours of negotiation the suspect drove to the police station and turned himself in.

I was once called to examine a murder scene at a house where a man had suffered fatal head injuries in an assault by a family member. I was told that a known suspect, who remained at large, had attacked the victim with an axe.

The old villa had at least seven vehicles parked on the front lawn. The back yard was littered with rubbish, car parts and all sorts of other discarded items. Inside, the house had a neglected look, with furnishings dating back to the 1970s and more car parts scattered around. There were two bedrooms, one with a double bed and the other with bunk beds. Neither room had much in the way of furniture, and the beds were not made up. The wooden floor was dotted with a few worn rugs.

In the living room a two-piece suite was draped with blankets, and the small wooden coffee table was cluttered with overflowing ashtrays and empty bottles. In the far corner, beneath a window, was another double bed, piled with blankets and pillows. In the midst of this chaotic heap, the outline of a person's head was visible, with blood staining the covers and seeping onto the mattress. On the floor near the door lay a large axe, its wooden handle heavily bloodstained. Blood droplets led from the axe back to the bed.

There were stepping plates down, because the wooden floor displayed clear signs of blood staining, as well as the potential for footwear and footprint evidence. Additionally, the bloodied axe obviously required examination for fingerprints, blood, and any hair or other trace evidence. I first packaged the axe, using two large exhibit boxes and securing the axe with garden wire, for future examination in the lab by both ESR and the fingerprint section.

Next I examined the living-room floor, starting by sampling the blood droplets with sterile swabs. I then applied white fingerprint powder to the wooden floor to develop any footwear or footprints. Clear ridge detail was apparent from people walking barefoot. I preserved the developed impressions using a specialist type of gel developed for uneven surfaces and woodgrain.

With the living-room floor and hallway cleared, we could safely remove the stepping plates. This allowed us to examine the space around the bed and the body without the risk of tripping or, God forbid, inadvertently falling on the body itself. We carefully removed the bedding from around the body and placed it in paper exhibit bags for further analysis by ESR. The axe had inflicted severe damage to the victim's head, including penetrating the back of the skull, resulting in a significant open fracture.

After the body was photographed from various angles, the body could then be removed to the mortuary. We cleared a section of the floor and the exhibits officer began to open a body bag. At this point it appeared that the injuries to the victim were localised, meaning moving the body would be straightforward. He was a small man, so it would only take the two of us to lift him. I positioned myself to lift the shoulder area, while the exhibits officer prepared to take hold of the legs. As we began to lift, we suddenly heard a crack coming from the skull. The two sides of the skull were parting, exposing the damaged brain beneath. I rapidly lowered the shoulders back onto the bed and grasped the sides of the head with both hands, pushing them back together.

'Get some tape!' I said to the exhibits officer, who lowered the victim's legs back to the bed and ran to his kit. He wrapped tape around the top of the skull to hold it in place. 'Great reflexes, Tom!' the exhibits officer remarked, acknowledging my quick response. With the head secured, we got the body in the bag and I examined the rest of the premises.

I preserved another twenty finger and palm prints, using basic white and black powder techniques. I also used the chemical dye amido black to enhance the visibility of blood staining I had noticed on the walls and door frames in the living room and hallway. These I then photographed.

Following my examination, I met with the lead investigator to share my findings and get an update on the investigation. Preliminary conclusions were that there had been an argument between family members. One had fetched the axe from a garden shed and returned to assault the victim in his bed. The suspect remained at large, but police were confident he wouldn't be for long.

Back in the lab, the bloodstained axe required a series of specialised sequential treatments to recover various types of trace evidence. The first step was to record any signs of fingerprint detail within the blood. There is no evidence like bloody fingerprints on the alleged murder weapon. The next phase required me to take the axe to ESR, where any hairs and fibres would be collected and preserved. A specialist blood pattern analysist would also document the blood patterns on both blade and handle, taking blood samples for further analysis.

At this point, I returned the axe to the forensic laboratory to enhance the bloodstained ridge detail using amido black. The handle then underwent treatment with a wet chemical known as 1,2 indandione, which reacts with the amino acids released in sweat that have been absorbed by the wood. I then applied a forensic light source to fluoresce the fingerprints, allowing me to capture clear images using a specialised camera and filter. As a final step, to ensure I had uncovered as much evidence as possible, I treated the axe with ninhydrin to develop any fingerprints that may not have reacted to indandione.

Needless to say, these complex forensic procedures are often underplayed in fictional crime scene shows. We work a lot harder than they do!

The fingerprints found inside the house and on the axe identified the individual police had by then arrested. The suspect was tried at the High Court and found not guilty of murder by reason of insanity. He was diagnosed as schizophrenic and detained indefinitely in a secure mental health facility.

To conclude this chapter, I want to share an experience from the examination of a sexual violation scene. These offences are comparable to homicides in terms of their profound impact on victims and their families. The emotional and psychological scars can last a lifetime, affecting people's lives in ways that are difficult to fully comprehend if you have not been there. In this case, the victim was left deeply traumatised by her encounter with the intruder. She never regained her sense of safety, living in constant fear of being alone, and even the simple freedom of leaving her window open at night for fresh air was lost to her forever.

The incident took place at a rest home, where an assailant entered through an open window and violated an elderly woman in her bed.

At the scene I first inspected the window and its frame, before applying black powder using a specialised fingerprint brush known as a zephyr. Comprising thousands of pure glass fibres, this brush is exceptionally soft and ensures optimal absorption of the powder. As I worked, I felt goosebumps on my arms as clear fingerprints began to emerge on the inside surface of the frame. Their positioning, clarity and ridge detail showed definitively that they had been made by someone climbing in through the window.

I had the bedspread sent to ESR to test for semen, as the woman said the perpetrator had sat naked on the bed. This test initially involves a spray application of acid phosphate. It is a presumptive test, meaning a positive result does not confirm the presence of semen, but indicates the possibility. Further testing is then required to confirm the presence of semen before it can be sampled for DNA profiling.

I continued my examination, obtaining a few additional fingerprint lifts from the bedframe and set of drawers under the bed.

Back at the police station, I registered the fingerprints in the police forensic computer system before heading to the AFIS suite to search against the national database. The clarity of the prints was impressive, and within just two minutes the system returned 30 potential matches. I pulled up the first one and bingo! I could see that the print from the crime scene matched the fingerprint on screen. This was one of those gratifying moments when I realised that, at that point, no one else but me knew the identity of the suspect.

I pulled his details from the database and continued comparing his fingerprints with the lifts from the crime scene. Within an hour I had matched all the prints to this individual. I verified my identifications with two other fingerprint examiners, then called the investigating sergeant to share the news.

Relieved and excited, he issued an arrest warrant, and within two days the man was arrested. Ultimately he pleaded guilty not only to this crime but also to three other offences in the area.

Chapter 11

Chocolate Sauce and Campylobacter

While on call, I could be summoned at any hour, day or night. I have been woken up numerous times to attend serious crime scenes, to ensure that crucial evidence is preserved. One evening, around eight o'clock, I was called to another murder scene over 220 kilometres away in the Far North. The lead investigator, whom I knew well, told me the scene was secure but asked if I could travel up urgently to assist. I told her I would get there as early as I could the next morning. I packed a kit bag for four days and rang my colleague Ockert to ask whether he wanted to assist with the examination.

Early the next morning, Ockert and I travelled north, arriving around 11:00a.m. We headed straight to the incident room, where about twenty other officers were already assembled.

The briefing began with the lead investigator explaining, 'At approximately 5:30 p.m. the previous evening, friends of the victim became concerned when she didn't answer the door.

They entered through the back door and found her unresponsive on the living-room floor. Police were called, and upon arrival, uniformed officers secured the scene, as it was immediately apparent the woman was deceased.'

She continued. 'While securing the area, the police received a call about a suspicious individual in a garden down the road from the murder scene. He has since been arrested for trespassing.' The entire room, me included, was listening intently. 'The arrested individual is only seventeen years old. At this time we have no evidence linking him to the crime scene, so it will be your responsibility to investigate any potential connections.'

Several officers then shared their findings from overnight investigations. Then the lead investigator assigned tasks to team members and we dispersed.

Ockert and I drove to the crime scene, which was just five minutes away. A crowd had gathered outside the cordoned-off area, and people were laying flowers near the police tape close to the house. News crews from across New Zealand were also present, eager to capture footage and images of the scene and officers in PPE searching for clues. The police had set up a crime scene tent in front of the property, to serve as a place to store forensic equipment and for officers to change into PPE before entering the scene.

I parked next to the tent and we went to meet the rest of the crime scene team: an exhibits officer, two ESR staff, a photographer and two additional uniformed officers. It was at this point that an ESR staff member told us the scene was to be treated under LCN procedures.

As always, the only tools I relied on in the first instance were my eyes, my digital camera, and my trusty notebook and pen. After putting on full PPE, Ockert and I entered the single-storey house. The front entrance was obstructed by a large storage container, so we decided to access the property through the back door.

Metallic stepping plates led from outside the rear door into a small, enclosed hallway-style area. Off this, another door opened into the kitchen, which featured 1970s-style cabinets, linoleum flooring and an electric stove. Various food items sat on the bench, along with some partially made sandwiches. The main living area led off the kitchen, and directly in front of us lay the elderly victim.

She was lying on her back on the carpet, her arms outstretched. A blanket covered her from the waist down, and her upper clothing had been pushed up to her neck. A dining chair from the adjacent table had been placed over her head up to her nose. What initially appeared to be blood on her face was later identified as chocolate sauce, which had been poured over her. Behind her head the carpet was stained with blood, indicating a significant injury.

When confronted with any lifeless body at a crime scene, my subconscious goes into overdrive, grappling with thoughts about the person's final moments, and the fear they must have felt. I started to feel anger, but I know from experience that such responses, while human and natural, can cloud my judgement and obstruct the clarity I need to do my job. So I tried to push those feelings to the back of my mind and focus on doing a professional job.

I looked around the living room. The fireplace and sofas seemed untouched and the curtains were drawn, casting the room in dim light. A narrow hallway led to the bedrooms, bathroom and front door. One of the bedrooms contained two neatly made-up single beds, suggesting the victim may have been expecting guests. One small room had been converted into a sewing area and was filled with various types of haberdashery.

In the main bedroom a double bed was positioned against the far wall, with a set of drawers either side, both stacked with magazines. On the wall opposite, two large sets of drawers contained clothing. The bed was neatly made but showed signs of disturbance, indicating that someone had recently sat on its edge. On top of the bed lay a heavily bloodstained jumper, from which blood was transferring onto the bed cover.

After my initial visual examination I went outside to discuss strategy with my colleagues. With no suspect in the frame at this stage, I planned to examine the exterior of the house first, looking for signs of forced entry and fingerprints.

Ockert and I began examining the outsides of the windows to determine whether anyone had tried to climb through or even peered inside. One thing we were looking for was so-called 'writer's palm' impressions, which are those left by the sides of the palms of people who position their hands at the sides of their heads to peer through a window. The examination might also reveal impressions of other facial features, such as the forehead, nose and lips, which can then be swabbed for DNA.

This is exactly what we found on the living-room window. White fingerprint powder clearly showed both left-hand and right-hand writer's palms, and in the centre was a clear impression of someone's forehead, nose and lips. I preserved the ridge detail of the hands and swabbed the facial features for DNA profiling. Continuing our examination of the windows, we developed clear ridge detail of a person's palm in several other locations, as well as a distinct impression on the white-painted wall next to the front door. The clarity of these impressions — how easily they developed with the application of powder — told me they had been deposited recently.

Recognising the significance of this find, I decided to do something I'd not done before. After developing the palm print to its optimum level, and attaching an exhibit label and sticky forensic tape for measurement alongside, I photographed the print on my digital camera, then borrowed a laptop from the investigative team and emailed the image to a colleague in the fingerprint section to search against the database. Then I returned to my examination.

Since the rear door would serve as the main entry point during the examination, I decided to concentrate my efforts in this area next to prevent any loss of evidence. Latent fingerprints could easily be inadvertently wiped away by the fabric of our PPE suits as we brushed past when entering and leaving the property.

I was able to develop additional ridge detail from the palm area of an individual's hand, the positioning of which suggested that someone had recently entered through the back door. I preserved these with gel and placed them on acetate sheeting. Given that part of the examination required LCN sampling for biological cellular material, it was crucial to use a specialised sterile brush and powder. These items were packed separately and stored away from the rest of the equipment to avoid contamination. Each powder container and brush were labelled with a serial number, which we recorded in our documentation. After the examination these were disposed of immediately.

About three hours after emailing the palm print to the fingerprint section, a colleague rang with promising news. They had matched the palm print to that of a seventeen-year-old youth from the area. I relayed this information to the lead investigator, who was thrilled. It turned out the suspect was already in custody for an unrelated crime. The investigative team now had evidence to question the suspect in relation to the murder.

By now, the body had been at the scene for 24 hours and needed to be bagged and sent to the pathologist. This case was particularly unusual, as the victim had not only suffered physical injuries but also had cooking oil and chocolate sauce poured over her face and body by someone who appeared to have placed a chair over the top of her in order to sit down while doing so.

When the body was moved, it became clear the victim had suffered severe blunt force trauma to the back of the head. We wrapped the deceased in a large white plastic sheet, rolling it tightly to prevent any movement during the five-hour journey to Auckland.

At this point, evening was drawing in, so it was decided to close the scene down till the following day.

We attended the morning briefing at the station to hear the latest updates. Thanks to the identification of the palm print, the team now had a lead suspect, which allowed them to hold him in custody for longer. After the meeting, Ockert and I returned to the crime scene to continue our examination.

We next inspected the kitchen floor, so the stepping plates could be safely removed. After we applied magnetic powder to the lino with a magna brush, several different types of footwear impression began to develop. Among these was a print from a bare foot. The ridge detail was faint and unclear, but Ockert patiently reapplied the powder, layer upon layer, until the pattern emerged with enough clarity to be preserved for later comparison.

We set about examining items on the kitchen worktops, then investigated some bags that had been found in the hallway next to the blocked front door. From these, it was clear that the suspect had been in the process of removing items from the property. As I sifted through the bags, the assortment of items suggested we were dealing with an unusual individual. One of the bags contained empty rice bran oil and chocolate sauce bottles, the contents of which had been poured over the victim as she lay on the floor. The bag also held several items that were stained with blood, including the victim's glasses and a remote control for the television. The suspect was removing as much evidence as they could.

Another bag contained a random collection of low-value oddities taken from the house. I developed numerous fingerprints from these items, and preserved the bloodstained items for laboratory analysis.

The following morning I woke with severe stomach pains and nausea. I initially brushed it off, attributing it to my irregular eating and drinking habits over the past couple of days. Ockert and I returned to the house for a third day, hoping to wrap up our examination so we could get back to the laboratory and dive into analysing the evidence we had collected. We examined the rest of the living room, the bedrooms and bathroom, acquiring an additional fifteen finger and palm prints.

Meanwhile, the pain in my stomach had not eased; in fact, it became more intense as the day wore on.

One of the most inconvenient moments during a crime scene examination is when nature calls. The need to find a bathroom can be a logistical nightmare. First and foremost is the timing. Stopping for a toilet break in the middle of a forensic examination can feel a tad inappropriate, especially at a crucial part of the investigation.

Then there's the pressing question of where the nearest available bathroom might be. Obviously any facilities at the crime scene itself are out of bounds, so the next thing you hope for is an obliging neighbour. Failing that, you have to travel back to the nearest police station.

Then comes the cumbersome task of removing your PPE. In messy (i.e. bloody) scenes, this gear will often have been secured tightly around your hands and ankles with sticky tape. Yet full removal is essential in order to avoid contamination, which could compromise the safety of the public and other police. In short, it can be quite a while from when you feel the urge, to when you are finally able to relieve yourself.

Ockert and I finished examining the premises around 6 p.m. and briefed the lead investigator. As we began our drive back to Auckland, the pain in my stomach became so intense that Ockert pulled over several times to ask if I was okay. I wasn't. But I kept swallowing back the vomit because, with all the businesses along the route closed for the day, we couldn't find a restroom anywhere. In hindsight, of course, I realise I should have consulted a doctor before we left.

After five hours on the road we finally arrived at my house, which was about 45 kilometres north of Auckland. We were not supposed to go straight home after examining a major crime scene, because the continuity records should show that any evidence went directly from the scene to a secure police station. However, I was desperate, and, given my rural location, I felt it was unlikely anyone would steal the police vehicle containing the exhibits overnight.

Ockert assisted me into the house and advised Allie to get me a doctor as soon as possible. Allie reassured him. 'Don't worry, he can overreact when he is ill.' With that, Ockert left in his own car.

I remember very little of the next 24 hours — it's all a blur. By this time I was vomiting and had diarrhoea, and Allie told me later I looked as pale as a ghost. She helped me to bed, hoping a good night's sleep would see me right. When I still felt unwell the next morning, she called the police to arrange for the van to be collected. Within two hours, Ockert arrived with a colleague.

Before departing with the exhibits, they came to ask me for any instructions for examining the items in my absence. I apparently got out of bed to greet them and promptly collapsed on the floor and lost consciousness. They put me back into bed and considered calling an ambulance, but Allie insisted on driving me to hospital herself. By the time we arrived at A&E at North Shore Hospital I was incoherent, so I was admitted for testing.

I was diagnosed with a severe case of campylobacter and placed in isolation, with only Allie permitted to visit me. Over the next few days I received numerous medications and intravenous fluids to manage the infection. I remained in isolation for four days and then spent three more days in a standard ward before being cleared to return home.

After a further week I was well enough to return to work. There, I found that my colleagues had completed the analysis of the finger and palm prints from my last crime scene, as well as processing the exhibits collected. Out of the 30 fingerprints we developed, 24 were successfully matched to the suspect, including prints found on the bottle that had been identified as the weapon used to kill the elderly lady. We also identified him from the footprint taken from the kitchen floor, and biological swabs from the facial impressions on the outside of the living-room window.

The forensic pathologist concluded that the victim had been beaten before being struck multiple times on the back of the head with a bottle. During this brutal assault she sustained a broken arm, and several broken ribs and fingers, before ultimately succumbing to her injuries.

It was found that he had changed out of some of his clothing at the crime scene, donning the victim's late husband's dressing gown. He had then tried to clear evidence from the scene, placing items in the bags he subsequently left in the hallway.

He pleaded guilty to murder and was sentenced to life imprisonment with a minimum term of fifteen years.

Unfortunately, but unsurprisingly, the cases I remember best are often the more gruesome ones. This next one is one of those tragic situations that occur far too often, where someone loses control and lashes out at a family member, resulting in a devastating loss of life.

I was called to a murder scene involving the death of an 81-year-old man in his retirement flat, with a significant amount of blood present at the scene. Given that the location was some distance from Auckland, I prepared for a few days away from home. At the local police station I was told that investigators had identified three potential suspects, one of whom was the victim's close relative. I decided to visit the crime scene straight away to develop a forensic strategy for the scene examination.

The property was a single-storey end unit made of brick, likely constructed in the 1960s to accommodate elderly residents. It was raining, so the responding officers had set up a large blue tarpaulin over the front entrance. I entered through the back door, which was sheltered by a porch and had stepping plates set out. The door opened directly into a small, somewhat dated kitchen that was surprisingly clean and orderly, with everything neatly in its designated place.

I walked through the kitchen into the living room, where the elderly man lay on his back on the floor near the front door. More stepping plates had been arranged around the body to avoid disturbing the substantial area of blood staining on the carpet to one side of the body. On the other side a sofa was set against the wall, and directly opposite stood an old box-style television and radio.

The man's eyes were wide open and his face was covered in blood. His throat had been slit from one side to the other, the injury so severe, his head had almost been removed from his torso. Behind his head lay a brass statue. It too was heavily stained with blood, and was likely used to inflict at least some of the injuries.

Mixed in with the extensive blood staining on the carpet were bone fragments, though I was not yet able to determine their source. Low-level arterial blood spray had reached the inside surface of the front door, so I was pleased the door had been protected by a tarpaulin. Not only would this protect the scene from the weather, but it would also preserve the critical evidence on the inside surface of the door and floor.

Continuing with my initial walkthrough, I entered a single bedroom that was sparsely furnished with an unmade bed and a set of drawers. Opposite this room was a grubby bathroom and toilet, a surprising contrast to the clean kitchen.

Returning to the kitchen, I observed blood staining on the outside of what turned out to be a cutlery drawer. The inside surface of the sink also showed signs of blood staining and splashing.

I went outside to share my initial thoughts with the lead investigator and talk about how I might proceed. The investigator told me the three suspects they were focusing on were the victim's relative, her older boyfriend, and the boyfriend's daughter. The three had been seen leaving the property together shortly before the body was discovered.

Obviously these individuals had legitimate access to the property and had likely visited the victim multiple times prior to the murder, so their prints would be everywhere. The primary goal of this forensic examination, therefore, was to identify any prints or blood traces from the suspects on items that may have been used to inflict the injuries. Additionally, it was crucial to locate any vehicles they may have used after the murder, to examine them for traces of the victim's blood.

Other key evidence would come from the clothing and

footwear worn by the suspects during the assault. Given the amount of blood at the scene, it was highly likely that some had transferred to the perpetrators.

I carefully removed the tarpaulin from the front door and began a forensic fingerprint examination using basic black and white powder, applying them with a squirrel and a zephyr brush. I developed and preserved a number of finger and palm prints. I found no usable prints on the outsides of the windows, but several on the back door and in the porch area.

In the kitchen I observed faint blood staining on the lino floor. I applied acid violet, a chemical similar to acid black, which reacts with the protein in blood to enhance detail. Using a laboratory pipette, I carefully applied the chemical while making sure I didn't get any on the surrounding surfaces. This revealed distinctive patterns from blood-contaminated footwear — block and triangular shapes similar to those of a trainer.

After I had labelled and scaled the findings, the police photographer captured images. To complete the examination of the kitchen floor I applied black powder to uncover any additional impressions, which I lifted using a specialised footwear gel and preserved on acetate sheeting.

I removed the bloodstained cutlery drawer and placed it in a large exhibit box for analysis in the laboratory. Next, I examined the kitchen work surfaces, using black powder to uncover any additional fingerprints.

At this point we needed to remove the body from the scene. Because of the severity of the injuries, which included extensive open wounds, we once again opted for our standard white plastic sheeting. It offered far greater security and containment than the generic black zippered body bags so often portrayed in crime shows.

To prevent contaminating the sheeting with blood from the floor, we laid it out well away from the body. In this small room we could not open the sheet out completely as there was not enough room, so we laid it out with the edges rolled up to minimise exposure to contaminants. The exhibits officer and I then lifted the body from the floor, making sure to support the head.

Despite our best efforts, blood continued to seep from the victim's injuries, dripping onto the floor and the lower parts of our legs and booties. Our gloved hands were covered in blood from the back of the head. We wrapped the edges of the sheeting around the body to ensure minimal movement during transportation. The end result always reminded me of a morbid type of Christmas cracker — one you would definitely not want to open.

The ESR blood spatter expert assessed the blood patterns on the inside of the front door and adjacent wall. We analysed the large blood stains on the carpet and preserved all bone fragments for the forensic pathologist. The bloodstained statue was packed tightly in a box. I then completed my fingerprint examination in the living room, hallway, bedroom and bathroom, preserving several finger and palm prints.

It had been a long and exhausting day, but we were not

quite finished. As darkness fell, it was the perfect opportunity to process the interior of the crime scene with luminol to detect any blood stains that were not visible to the naked eye. Luminol is typically applied in a spray form, and the resulting fluorescence from the chemical reaction with iron in haemoglobin lasts for only about 30 seconds. The application therefore involves several stages. When the luminol is first sprayed, if a reaction occurs, the area is noted and a marking label prepared. The chemical is then reapplied to the same spot to confirm the reaction. At this point the label is attached, and the photographer quickly positions themselves to capture the reaction using a specialised filter on the camera. Luminol is then applied one last time to allow the photographer to document the detail.

The subsequent luminol applications do not alter the appearance of the blood stains. If a particularly significant area is identified, it is even possible to swab that location in order to try to obtain a DNA profile from the biological fluid.

The luminol process is generally repeated in other rooms of the property, where it sometimes reveals surprising evidence, such as the fact that a body has been moved.

At this scene the luminol reacted in several areas, including the kitchen sink, suggesting that the suspects washed their hands after the assault, as well as on several kitchen worktops. Additional reactions were observed in the living room, but there were no notable reactions in the bedroom or bathroom.

I never tire of watching the reaction of luminol and the

stunning effects it produces on surfaces that appear clean and uncontaminated.

I walked through the house once more to ensure that every space had been thoroughly assessed. I also made sure to wipe down all locations where finger and palm prints had been developed, to eliminate any remaining residue.

Back at the station I was told that one suspect had been arrested earlier that afternoon, and another had been detained while attempting to flee. Their clothing had been seized, preserved in paper bags (rather than plastic, to ensure they did not sweat and degrade), and set aside to accompany us down to Auckland for forensic examination.

The following morning I travelled to the Far North Search and Rescue centre to examine the two vehicles that had allegedly been used by the suspects to flee the crime scene. The first, a silver Mitsubishi Pajero, had certainly seen better days. The entire vehicle was filthy, inside and out, and the seat covers were torn. The boot was cluttered with old tools and clothing.

The other vehicle was a Mitsubishi Mirage, which was in even worse condition. It looked as if someone had been living inside it, with clothes and other belongings scattered across the back seat. The exterior paint was severely cracked and peeling, and most of the metal components were rusted beyond repair. I wondered how on earth it could still be on the road.

As you can imagine, it is quite challenging to lift prints from cars in this condition, as they have few clean surfaces that might have latent prints. However, I was pleasantly surprised to find that I got some very clear prints from various surfaces of both vehicles.

The seats were taped to collect hairs and fibres, and the interior surfaces closely examined for traces of blood. To estimate the height of the person who last drove each vehicle, I measured the distance from the accelerator pedal to the base of the driver's seat. This can provide an indication of the driver's foot length, which in turn can help estimate their height.

In order to use luminol to detect hidden blood, the vehicles were moved inside a windowless work shed to create darkness. Small traces of blood were detected in the driver's footwell of the Pajero, and samples collected for analysis.

Examinations complete, we all assembled in the briefing room to present our findings to the team. During this meeting we also discussed which exhibits should be prioritised for examination, focusing on those most likely to yield valuable forensic information. Such triage is crucial in serious crime investigations where the number of exhibits can reach into the hundreds. It is neither practical nor feasible to analyse all of them simultaneously.

Back in Auckland, my top priority was to evaluate the finger and palm prints collected from the crime scene and the vehicles. Since suspects had already been detained, comparing the collected prints with their prints was straightforward.

In the laboratory I examined the brass statue, looking particularly for any ridge detail that may be present within the blood. Unfortunately, there was not enough for a conclusive comparison. However, blooded samples were collected from the statue for DNA profiling, and ESR analysed the blood spatter to determine the directionality of the blood droplets, in order to assess how the statue might have been used to create the victim's injuries.

ESR also examined the clothing taken from the suspects, recording details about blood transfer from the victim and noting the direction and amount of blood, which provided insights into the amount of force applied during the attack.

Three individuals were eventually charged with murder and appeared before the High Court at Auckland. During the trial it was alleged that the victim's relative struck him on the head, while her boyfriend stabbed him multiple times. The boyfriend's daughter then inflicted the cut to the victim's throat that nearly decapitated him.

The court found that the two women were both legally insane at the time of the crime, rendering them incapable of standing trial. They were committed to a secure mental health facility.

The male defendant, however, was found guilty of murder. The evidence against him included blood discovered on his boots and clothing, as well as fingerprints found within the house and one of the vehicles. He was sentenced to life imprisonment, with a minimum non-parole period of thirteen years.

Chapter 12
The Christchurch Earthquake of 2011

The world had always been beset with disasters, and victim identification processes now are much more effective than they used to be. During the American Civil War (1861–65), soldiers often took it upon themselves to ensure they could be identified if they fell in battle. They would make agreements with fellow soldiers to note each other's burial sites and inform families. Many soldiers carried personal identifiers, such as slips of paper with their names on, or letters.

Fast-forward to 1881, and a devastating fire swept through the Ring Theatre in Vienna, Austria, claiming 449 lives. Thanks to very early forensic autopsy and DVI techniques, 284 of these victims could be identified.

Closer to home, on 28 November 1979 a sightseeing Air New Zealand flight crashed into Mt Erebus on Ross Island, Antarctica. All 257 on board were killed. This recovery marked a pivotal moment in the development of DVI, with the establishment of Operation Overdue, in which multiple teams of experts worked in twelve-hour shifts to meticulously document, preserve and collect all human remains. The remains were transported to Whenuapai Air Force Base in Auckland, where they were taken to a mortuary for identification. The process took several weeks, but the team successfully identified 213 of the 257 victims. The 44 unidentified victims were laid to rest in sixteen caskets at Waikumete Cemetery in West Auckland on 22 February 1980.

Nowadays, international DVI teams are mobilised to handle both open and closed disasters. Closed disasters are those such as aircraft accidents, where the number of casualties can be determined immediately. Open disasters are typically caused by unpredictable events such as earthquakes, wildfires, floods or large-scale terrorist attacks, where the exact number of casualties is initially unknown.

At lunchtime on 22 February 2011, I was at work in the forensic fingerprint section in Auckland. The office was its usual hive of activity as staff worked cases ranging from vehicle theft to murder.

A little after 2 p.m., reports began to trickle in of a magnitude 6.3 earthquake that had just struck the Canterbury region. Earthquakes are not uncommon in New Zealand and my colleagues and I carried on with our work, though I do remember thinking at the time, wow, they had a magnitude 7.1 quake only six months ago.

Soon, however, the boss emerged from his office to tell us that significant damage had been reported in Christchurch's CBD and surrounding areas. At that time there was no confirmed news of injuries. By now we had a radio tuned to a news station, which was broadcasting live updates about the quake and its aftermath from eyewitnesses.

'Not looking good down there, is it?' a colleague remarked as he manoeuvred through the small crowd that had gathered around the radio. The first reports indicated extensive building damage but no fatalities. With that, some of my co-workers and I wrapped up our work and made our way home at the end of our early shift.

As I drove home from work, the rhythmic beats of one of my favourite songs filled the car, creating a cocoon of familiar comfort amid the monotonous crawl of Auckland traffic. Then, mid-song, a news alert. The announcer's voice was sharp and urgent.

'We interrupt our regular programming to bring you breaking news. There are confirmed reports that persons have died from falling debris during the earthquake within the central business district of Christchurch. We will provide more updates as they become available.'

The music returned, but my mind lingered on the gravity of the report. I glanced around at the sea of cars inching along the road, my concern growing. Each moment of my journey felt heavier as I thought about the impact of another disaster on the already-stricken Canterbury region.

I remember the familiar click of the front door unlocking as I pushed it open and stepped into the quiet sanctuary of my home. I tossed my bag, coat and keys onto the floor in a heap and my fingers fumbled to flick on the TV. The screen came to life almost immediately, broadcasting live footage from the streets of Christchurch. I stood frozen, my eyes riveted to the images unfolding before me. The scenes were chaotic: people stumbling through debris, their faces a mix of confusion and fear, their movements disoriented.

The camera panned across the devastation, the operator clearly struggling to decide where to focus amid the overwhelming destruction. The scale of the damage was staggering, and the footage conveyed a palpable sense of helplessness. It was as if the enormity of the disaster had left everyone on the ground — citizens and news crew — stunned and adrift.

As I watched, a knot tightened in my chest. The normalcy of my day felt like a distant memory, now overshadowed by what was happening in Christchurch, with reports emerging of further fatalities and multiple injuries. I knew at this point that a disaster response would be required. I was jolted from my focus by Allie walking into the living room. 'You're home early,' I said. I had been so absorbed in the news that I hadn't realised two hours had passed since I started watching.

'It's looking really bad in Christchurch, isn't it?' Allie said as she picked up my coat and bag from the floor and put them away.

My mobile phone started ringing but I kept staring at the TV screen.

'Are you going to answer that?' asked Allie.

I picked up the call to hear my boss on the other end. He told me a DVI team was being assembled for deployment, and my name was on the list of first responders. The commissioner was coordinating the teams and managing the logistical details of the operation. I was instructed to prepare a kit bag and await further instructions while they worked out the travel arrangements and the status of Christchurch Airport.

The rest of the evening was a blur as I organised my gear while keeping up with live updates on TV3 and TV1, both of which had replaced their usual programming with coverage of the earthquake.

When my boss finally called, he instructed me to be at Auckland Central Police Station by 7 a.m. 'Don't be late — we're being flown to Christchurch by the air force,' he said. I knew commercial flights into Christchurch had been suspended.

A chill ran down my spine. I had handled many DVI responses before, but this was on an unprecedented scale for New Zealand. Furthermore, aftershocks were still shaking the region. It all felt unpredictable and perilous.

That night was interminable as I lay sleepless, my mind racing with concerns about leaving my wife and daughter and the horrific scenes I might face upon arrival.

In the morning I had just 45 hectic minutes to manage everything — shit, shower and shave, then dress in my police-issued DVI uniform, which consisted of boots, T-shirt and blue army-style trousers. Allie double-checked my kit bag, making sure I had two boiler-style police overalls, spare T-shirts, toiletries, and a few items of comfort food.

At 6 a.m. I grabbed my kit bag, kissed Allie goodbye, and hugged Hannah, who was crying. In a soft whisper, she said, 'Please be careful, and come home soon. I love you.'

I had assumed the traffic on SH1 southbound would be clear at that hour but I was sorely mistaken. For about 3 kilometres it was at a standstill. 'Bollocks,' I muttered in frustration. 'How the hell am I going to get through this?' There was no way I would make it in time.

I called 111 and explained my situation to the operator. She dispatched a marked unit to assist me and I received permission from the acting inspector at the call centre to use the breakdown lane of the motorway, provided I kept my lights on full. I proceeded as permitted, no doubt to the annoyance of the many drivers stuck in the traffic.

I pulled up just after 7 a.m. to be greeted by five colleagues. Before I could utter a word, one of them shouted, 'No time to explain; we need to get to Whenuapai right away.' They hurled their kit bags into the boot of my ageing Volvo 440 and three of my colleagues climbed in with me. The other two travelled in the marked police car parked ahead of me.

'Just follow the police car and keep up!' one of my colleagues bellowed.

The police car roared off, lights flashing and sirens wailing, cutting a path through the traffic. I cranked up the Volvo to follow. 'Hurry up, Tom, put your foot down! We don't want to lose them!'

For the next twenty minutes I chased the marked car through rush-hour traffic, trying desperately to keep pace. The Volvo strained to keep up as we barrelled through the congested streets at an average speed of 100 km/h.

When we arrived at Whenuapai, my poor car felt like it might fall apart at any moment, like a clown car in a circus — doors dropping off and bonnet primed to shoot into the sky. Stepping out of it, I couldn't shake a sense of the absurdity of the situation.

As we grabbed our bags, the weight of the moment settled in. The base was a hum of activity, and an Air Force Boeing 757 was waiting on the tarmac. The engine noise pierced the tension, the roar loud amid the quiet unease that hung in the air.

Within minutes we were airborne, with an estimated flight time of 1 hour 30 minutes. This being an RNZAF plane, there were no flight attendants offering drinks or snacks from a trolley. In fact the interior of the aircraft was worn and tired, lacking the modern amenities we expect of air travel.

All aircraft on the ground at Christchurch Airport were being mobilised for evacuating people from the surrounding areas. We were swiftly directed into a waiting police vehicle and driven into the heart of the CBD. The scene outside the car windows was reminiscent of a war zone. From the safety of our vehicle I could see the devastation first hand: homes that once sheltered families had crumbled into towering heaps of rubble, with smoke and dust still swirling in the air. I later learned that this north-west side of town had suffered much less damage than the south and east.

The ground was covered in a thick grey substance we were told was due to liquefaction, whereby water-saturated sediment loses its strength and surfaces as grey silt and mud. Christchurch streets were covered with it. Uniformed army personnel lined the streets, assisting in evacuations and maintaining cordons around the most severely impacted areas.

After 30 minutes of navigating along debris-strewn, pot-holed roads, we finally arrived at our dropoff point in the city centre. We donned hard hats and made our way to the makeshift police command centre. Inside, uniformed officers, search and rescue teams, army personnel and paramedics awaited orders from senior officers overseeing this complex operation.

At this stage the main focus was life preservation and rescue efforts. As our specialist role was DVI, we knew we had to take a back seat initially, allowing other agencies to perform life-critical tasks throughout the city and its surrounding areas. It was a whirlwind of organised chaos; every person on the ground was constantly receiving updated information, and being assigned specific tasks based on their expertise.

During these disaster events the waiting is hard. I hate watching others rush around being busy when I can do nothing. Then it happened: my first-ever earthquake. I heard a distant rumble that quickly grew louder, and suddenly the ground began to shift beneath me. Time seemed to slow down. My legs turned to jelly, wobbling uncontrollably as the sensation travelled up my body, through my arms and into my hands. My entire body shook from side to side. Grabbing onto something for stability proved futile, as it swayed in rhythm. I later found out the tremor was only magnitude 4.2, and lasted only a few seconds, but to me it brought a terror that I will never forget.

Then there was a job for us to do. We were to go to the mortuary to examine three bodies found unresponsive on the street. They had been taken to Christchurch Hospital but pronounced dead upon arrival. The hospital was only a five-minute walk away so we quickly gathered our examination kits and set off. Nestled between South Hagley Park and the city's Botanic Gardens stood a tired-looking building in desperate need of modernisation. Inside, most of the staff were busy evacuating patients to other facilities across the country.

The mortuary, located in the basement, reminded me of an old Victorian-style mortuary with its aged yellow-tiled walls and familiar overpowering smell of disinfectant mixed with the stench of decay that the air conditioning could never fully mask. In the centre of the room stood three vintage metal gurneys with the deceased peacefully lying upon them, covered in white sheets, offering a fragment of dignity.

Our role was to examine the victims' hands and feet to record their ridge detail. We had just begun when a faint rumbling reached our ears, quickly intensifying. Holy shit, I thought. The floor shook beneath us, and within seconds ceiling tiles began to crash to the ground, while the walls swayed. We dropped to the ground, gripping the gurneys as the bodies slid from side to side, caught in the chaos. 'This is fucking insane!' one of the group shouted. Within 30 seconds it subsided, and we began to pick ourselves up from the floor.

I had to agree; it really was madness. Here we were, trapped in the windowless basement of an ancient hospital, a concrete staircase our only means of escape.

We abandoned our work and returned to the command centre, explaining to our senior officer that it was far too dangerous to carry out such procedures in an enclosed, grave-like space during frequent aftershocks. After considerable debate, an army official suggested we use the military base at Burnham, which he said was safe and secure, and just outside Christchurch.

That afternoon a group of us visited Burnham military camp, where we were shown a large old wooden storage area, previously used for housing military vehicles and equipment. The army colonel who was showing us around suggested it could serve as a makeshift mortuary, and I could see its potential right away. One of our senior staff exclaimed, 'This is ideal. Can you have this up and running in 24 hours?' The response was blunt: 'It depends on what's required.' Then, without missing a beat, he added: 'Okay — shitloads.'

That night I stayed in one of the few hotels the government had commandeered in Christchurch for DVI personnel involved in all aspects of the DVI. The food was good and the beds comfortable, which was a relief amid the ongoing rumbling of aftershocks.

The next morning we were told that to save travelling time we would be staying on site at Burnham. This meant leaving the comfort of the hotel to spend the rest of our tour in army barracks, where I found myself sharing quarters with young soldiers. It was cramped, hectic and noisy. My space wasn't my own, and the shared showers and facilities took me back to the days of school camps.

The upside was that our barracks were just a two-minute walk from the makeshift mortuary. And what a difference 24 hours had made. Electricity cables hung from the ceiling and crisscrossed the floor, looking like snakes in motion. A row of empty gurneys waited at one end, ready to transport the deceased within the facility.

The space was divided into four sections, each equipped with tables, chairs and workstations. These sections represented the four phases of the PM DVI procedures. During this deployment the setup was somewhat different from my time in Thailand with the Boxing Day tsunami contingent. The bodies we were to examine this time would be relatively fresh, showing only early signs of decomposition, so they would be examined in the following order: photography, pathology, odontology, finger prints.

It was a sobering environment, filled with a sense of urgency and purpose. As I approached the building on the first day I was struck by the sight of a large green army tent at the entrance. This was our only way in, and also served as a changing area for DVI personnel to put on our gowns and white gumboots.

Passing through the tent, I could hear the low hum of several large refrigerated shipping containers brought in to slow the decomposition of the deceased within.

This was the first day all the DVI personnel from around the country came together, and it was a time filled with anticipation and fear of the unknown. Before we took our positions at our designated stations, we formed a circle just inside the mortuary. A local minister and an iwi tohunga — a Māori community representative — led us in a heartfelt prayer, spoken in both English and te reo Māori. Regardless of our individual beliefs, I think the moment resonated deeply with everyone. The deafening silence spoke volumes about the solemn duty we were about to undertake.

I was stationed in phase four of the process, tasked with recording the best possible fingerprints, palm prints and footprints using the variety of techniques at our disposal. The four of us worked in two teams of two. The first worked in what we called the 'dirty section', handling the deceased and likely to find themselves covered in biological fluids. The second pair worked in the 'clean section', focused on completing the paperwork on the pink DVI PM forms. The teams rotated daily. This system not only fostered teamwork but also provided us all with a deeper understanding of the whole process we were all part of.

As each body was removed from the storage container and placed on a waiting gurney, the minister offered a prayer while the tohunga performed a karakia, a traditional Māori blessing.

Witnessing this was one of the most moving experiences of my life. The minister and tohunga worked in seamless harmony, honouring each other's customs and traditions in a way that radiated mutual respect. At the conclusion of the process, the two also blessed every individual before they were returned to the containers, awaiting confirmation of their identities. This final act of reverence left a lasting impression on me, underscoring the importance of dignity and compassion in our work.

The containers held deceased transported from various locations around Christchurch. Meanwhile, reports were coming in of catastrophic damage to a building known as the CTV (Canterbury Television) building, which had collapsed in on itself, trapping many inside. The building had dropped like a stack of cards, and it was clear that reaching those trapped was going to involve a monumental effort. There were known to be fatalities and many injured, including with severe crush injuries.

Within a couple of hours we received our first victim. It appeared at the start to be a relatively straightforward examination, as the person had no missing limbs and was a 'fresh body', meaning there was minimal decomposition. I set about recording all eight fingers, both thumbs and the full palm area of the hands, using ink on the friction ridge detail and placing each onto a marked-out strip of finger and palm print paper. I handed these over to an officer in the 'clean section', who checked the prints for quality and then completed the paperwork.

The rest of the day unfolded without any particularly difficult aspects, but deep down our team understood that the challenges would intensify as time went on. At the end of the day we gathered to debrief and discuss any hurdles we had faced. This meeting at the end of each shift proved crucial; it allowed us to talk through any issues and ensure we were prepared for the next shift.

Then it was time for showers, to try to wash away the lingering smell of the mortuary. No matter how hard I scrubbed, it always felt as if the scent still clung to me. I often wondered whether it was just in my head or if I really did smell like death. I certainly wasn't brave enough to ask anyone. I sensed that others shared my discomfort.

The army canteen was basic but clean, serving up nourishing meals that were essential to maintaining our energy. One of the most important lessons I learned during my DVI training at the National Police Training Centre was the necessity of self-care. Staying hydrated and taking adequate breaks were crucial for our well-being, especially in such emotionally taxing circumstances.

We returned to our sleeping quarters, physically exhausted and mentally drained from the day's events. Before I slept, I called Allie and Hannah. Our conversations always felt strange in moments like this. I couldn't share the details of the day's work, as it would only distress them, rather than offer the comfort they were seeking. Instead, I let them guide the conversation. Hannah talked enthusiastically about her day at school, while Allie filled me in on her work. Allie had grown accustomed to these one-sided exchanges from my previous DVI deployments and long days at murder scenes. It was our way of staying connected despite the distance and the weight of what I was experiencing. Hearing their voices provided a sense of normalcy, reminding me of the life waiting for me beyond this current reality.

The soldiers whose barracks we were sharing were much younger than us and worked different shifts. Just as we had settled in for what we hoped would be a peaceful night's sleep, chaos erupted. At 11 p.m. some of the soldiers decided to throw a party, and cranked up their music to an ear-splitting volume. The bass thumped through the place, jolting me awake.

'What the fuck?!' I shouted, disoriented from my deep sleep.

I got out of bed and joined several colleagues who were already standing in the corridor, incensed at the soldiers' thoughtlessness. They knew who we were and what we were doing there. Just as we were about to confront them, the music suddenly stopped and one of our team members came over to reassure us. 'It's sorted,' he said. 'They won't be playing any more music tonight.' With a wave of relief, I returned to my bed.

The next morning, as I walked to the mortuary, the familiar grim smell came to meet me. It was being expelled from the cooling fans connected to the containers, which by now held the remains of well over 150 individuals.

We were setting up our workstation for the day when a commotion erupted at the security gates. An Israeli DVI response team had arrived unannounced, eager to assist. We already had teams from Australia, the UK, Thailand and China, and the unexpected presence of the Israelis raised a few questions among our team leaders.

It turned out that the Israeli team was equipped with state-of-the-art DVI equipment. Their forensic fingerprint resources made our equipment look prehistoric. In that moment, I realised we were not as well prepared as we had thought, but fortunately their specialist equipment would not be required for these examinations.

Over the next few days we examined around 40 bodies, gathering crucial PM data. Meanwhile, AM information was slowly being pulled together from across New Zealand and from various other countries. Both sets of data were checked and entered in databases, and DVI officers worked tirelessly to establish connections that could positively identify the victims. As the days passed, the mortuary process was working like clockwork, with each team working at maximum efficiency.

Even though the deceased were stored in temperature-controlled containers, the decomposition process continued, with some bodies entering the putrefaction stage before we got to them. To slow this process further it was decided to set some units to freezing, a choice that seemed logical at the time but, in hindsight, may not have been the best decision. Some bodies ended up completely frozen, forcing us to wait for them to defrost before we could begin our examinations.

As the bodies became increasingly moist from decomposition, we stopped using the fingerprint ink. Instead, we brushed specialised black fingerprint powder onto the fingers and palm of the deceased, lifting the prints with white sticky paper. Each print was then placed onto clear plastic sheeting, so everything was documented in reverse. This required you to think and act backwards, which is much more difficult than you might imagine. We had to make sure the sheet was flipped so the prints were in the correct order.

During one memorable shift, a forensic pathologist I knew well from previous DVI events called me over. He had just finished removing a victim's metal hip replacement and needed my help to read the unique serial number stamped on the item, which was either worn down or had been poorly stamped in the first place. It was nearly impossible to read.

Another officer and I spent the next couple of hours improvising a mini-darkroom. Inside it we used alternate light sources (ALS), the device mentioned earlier that breaks light into different frequencies, allowing us to see details invisible under normal lighting. As we examined the hip replacement under 415 nm and 555 nm, the worn serial number gradually emerged, allowing us to record it on the pink DVI form. We later learned that this information had served as a crucial identifier for the victim in question, helping to facilitate their release to loved ones.

As time passed, we began to receive body parts rather than full bodies coming through for examination. In the DVI process it's crucial not to make any assumptions. You can't simply match an odd limb with a body that might be missing one. Each piece must undergo the full DVI procedure to be absolutely certain of where it belongs.

By the third week we were exhausted, and at the end of

each shift all we wanted was a good meal, a chance to call our loved ones, and then sleep. But it was not that easy. A few of the younger soldiers clearly resented us taking over their space in the barracks, and their annoyance was growing. The constant music at all hours became a major issue.

One night, just as we were settling down, *boom!* Once more, loud bass music erupted through our sleeping quarters at 11 p.m. I could hear some of my colleagues shouting, 'For fuck's sake, turn that shit off! Can't you see we're knackered and want to sleep?!' Before long several soldiers showed up, ready for a showdown.

Just as fists were about to fly, the camp warden arrived and defused the situation. If he hadn't, who knows what would have happened. The next morning the colonel apologised to our team for the inconsiderate behaviour of a few of his personnel and assured us it wouldn't happen again.

By week four, we were almost finished. Most of the deceased had been identified. The remains, which had been in storage all this time, were gradually released to families, after a final blessing by the local minister and the tohunga. All of us in the mortuary stood in line, paying our final respects to those we had worked to bring back to their families. It was a solemn moment, and an honour to have played a part in the process.

It was time for us all to return to our regular duties, whether in the police, a mortuary, a dental surgery or within our local communities. The departure was emotional, with many of us struggling to hold back tears as we said our goodbyes. We had shared a unique and intense journey, behind the scenes and out of view of the public. For those of us who had been there, it had been an unforgettable rollercoaster of emotion, dedication and compassion.

Our team from Auckland were escorted back to Christchurch Airport, which had now reopened to domestic and international airlines. We boarded our Air New Zealand flight and travelled back in a little more style than we had arrived in. At the arrivals gate, Allie and Hannah enveloped me in hugs and kisses.

After a relaxing night, Allie drove me to Whenuapai to collect my car, which was still sitting in the spot I had left it in four weeks previously. The old Volvo was a little the worse for wear but still got me home.

In loving memory of those who died in the Christchurch earthquake of 2011:

New Zealand	97
Japan	28
China	23
Philippines	11
Thailand	6
Israel	3
Korea	2
Canada, Ireland, Malaysia, Peru, Romania, Russia, Serbia, Taiwan, Turkey and US	1 each
No nationality recorded	5

Chapter 13

Life After the Police

At the age of 49, I found myself reflecting on nearly three decades of service in the police in New Zealand and London. It had been a fulfilling journey, but I felt that if I stayed any longer I might become too comfortable and institutionalised — trapped in the same role for the rest of my working life.

I had at least another sixteen years of active work life before I reached retirement age, and I wanted to make sure those years were filled with new challenges and growth, rather than the same old same old. With a sense of determination, I decided to take the bold step of resigning from the New Zealand Police.

The move caught my managers completely off guard. And yet it was a decision that felt both liberating and necessary — a move to embrace new challenges and opportunities. In any role, no matter how good you are, there's always someone who can step in and fill your shoes.

Allie and I decided to leave Auckland behind and embark

on a journey as moteliers by purchasing a motel in Stratford, Taranaki. Hannah decided to stay in Auckland in her position as evening news editor for *Newshub*. The property featured ten self-contained rooms and a separate four-bedroom house, all spread across 2 hectares of picturesque, park-like grounds. While the setting was beautiful, the rooms themselves were dreary and outdated, requiring a complete makeover to meet the standards we envisioned.

Stepping into the hospitality industry was a significant career departure for both of us. Allie adapted remarkably well, taking to her new role like a duck to water. I, on the other hand, decided I was more comfortable in the background, handling the maintenance and gardening tasks, taking on a supportive role in our new venture.

After dedicating five months to refurbishing the rooms, I found myself becoming overly protective of them, giving short shrift to any guest who disrespected our hard work. I supposed I embodied the character of Basil Fawlty, pacing up and down the premises to ensure guests adhered to the motel's rules and regulations.

More often than I'd like to admit, I found myself treating guest rooms like crime scenes. It was disheartening to find sheets soiled with shit marks or blood, which I felt indicated a basic lack of respect for the property. On one occasion I found that someone had projectile-vomited all over the bathroom walls and left without telling us or trying to clean up the mess.

But most of our guests were very pleasant, decent people.

One of our regulars had a routine that became quite familiar over time. He would arrive early in the morning and head directly to his room. About ten minutes later another car would pull up, and a woman would discreetly enter the room. About two hours later they would leave separately, each returning to their own lives. Following their departure, I entered the room, cleaned and tidied after their romantic rendezvous, and collected the cash payment left behind. This remarkably efficient process allowed the room to be readied for another guest later that day. At times I did wonder what I was doing, spending my time facilitating this clandestine affair.

Maintaining a septic system in a rural motel presented its own, sometimes rather unpleasant, challenges. Our location meant we had no connection to the sewerage network so relied on a large septic tank, serving all rooms. Routine maintenance frequently involved encountering items in the system that absolutely should not have been flushed — used condoms, sanitary products, knickers and other such waste. The sheer volume of this inappropriate disposal was, frankly, astonishing, despite every toilet having clear signage. It did occur to me that DNA analysis could have identified the offenders . . .

I wasn't particularly enjoying being a motelier, but I recognised that Allie was thriving on it, and stuck with it as long as I could. Eventually, however, I chose to return to my roots and took on a position as a consultant for a well-regarded company. My role involved reassessing crime scenes and exhibits to ensure that the police and their experts had adhered to all necessary protocols and procedures. This required me to visit police stations and forensic laboratories to discuss findings with the fingerprint experts or crime scene examiners, and involved evaluations of their work.

While the police are expected to operate with transparency and honesty, my status as a former colleague sometimes meant I was perceived as an adversary, there solely to uncover flaws in their examinations. I often found myself reassuring them that my critiques were not personal, though some of my former colleagues saw it differently.

I have to say I was taken aback by the approach some scene examiners took to their work, including in some cases the lack of thoroughness.

I was called to court on one occasion by a lawyer representing a client charged with drug offences. My role was to sit in the courtroom and listen to the testimony from the exhibits officer and the scene examiner, to spot any procedural flaws. During a break I discussed some concerns with the lawyer. The lawyer then brought these issues to the judge's attention, requesting a Section 147 dismissal of charges based on my assessment. The judge agreed with the concerns raised and quashed the charges.

It was now the summer of 2019 and I was on my ride-on mower one day when I had a 'eureka' moment. Why didn't I teach forensic science to students? I shared my vision with Allie, enthusiastically describing how I could show them the 'real' CSI experience. Allie is normally a mild-mannered person. She heard me out, and then said in a calm voice: 'Fuck off.' I sensed at this point that she was perhaps not 100 per cent behind me.

'You've spent 30 years in forensic science,' she said, 'leaving behind a bloody good, well-paying job to come here, and you now want to teach it? What about the motel?'

I gently suggested we could maybe sell it, but my suggestion only seemed to increase her frustration.

'How are you going to set up a company down here in the middle of nowhere?' she continued, her voice raised slightly as if we were on the brink of an argument. When I mentioned the possibility of moving back to Auckland she left the room, closing the door just firmly enough to show her displeasure.

My vision was ambitious: a crime centre offering a realistic experience of crime scene investigation, encompassing the science and techniques involved. I envisaged mock crime scenes where participants could locate and develop forensic evidence, and then search a database for footwear, hair, fibre, DNA and fingerprint matches. To enhance the realism I wanted to incorporate an AFIS database, but at a cost of around $300 million I was a few dollars short. So I turned to Richard Kerry, a brilliant computer programmer and close friend. I explained my concept, and Richard, without hesitation, agreed to develop a customised system. He warned me it would take a while.

Over the next two weeks I drip-fed the details to Allie. I laid out my handwritten concepts — rough sketches, bullet points and priorities — and mapped how we could make it work without losing ourselves in the process. We spoke about money, timing and the sale of the motel. The plan only made sense on one setting: full commitment from both of us. We would be working as a team. Slowly her initial hesitation eased, and the path ahead looked possible. We agreed that it would involve moving back to Auckland, with its bigger population base.

Allie and I brainstormed names and settled on Forensic Insight, a title we felt captured the broad scope of forensic science we planned to cover. My enthusiasm surged, and I immediately began planning the logistics, including an initial team-building event. I also ordered a substantial amount of PPE — half a container load, to be exact! The delivery driver raised his eyebrows when he realised he was about to unload all this PPE at a motel. He clearly thought we were running something far more sinister.

I created a realistic training prop: a full-body mannequin with a remarkably lifelike head, sourced from a company in the US that specialised in film and TV props. The body was so real I had to prevent any accidental encounters with motel guests casually walking around our gardens.

In March 2020, life took a dramatic turn with the arrival of Covid-19. This pandemic profoundly impacted everyone, leaving no country untouched. On 25 March, New Zealand implemented a level-four lockdown, making it mandatory for everyone to stay at home unless they were confirmed as essential workers. Like countless other businesses, our motel was compelled to shut down for 32 days, relying on financial support provided by the government. I felt a bit bad when the media reported that hospitals, care centres and other establishments caring for others were running short of PPE for their staff members when I had a garage full of the stuff . . .

After New Zealand emerged from lockdown, our hospitality business, like most others, faced a significant downturn in customers. The situation was exacerbated when the border closed to tourists, with no clear indication of when things might change. For a challenging four months we relied heavily on government assistance to keep the business afloat. Then, even though it seemed a crazy time to market a hospitality business, we decided to take a chance and put the business up for sale.

Despite our significant investment in renovations and parkland upgrades, our specialist hospitality estate agent could not find a buyer, even after considerable marketing efforts. Then, in a surprising turn of events, in September 2020, two gentlemen who had booked a room for the night approached me with a cash offer. They wanted a simple transaction, bypassing the usual processes of surveys and estate agents. One of them handed me a piece of paper with their names, a contact number, and the amount they were willing to pay. A wave of excitement washed over me; I had feared being stuck in this situation for years, and the prospect of finally moving forward with Forensic Insight suddenly felt within reach.

Things progressed rapidly and we finalised the deal, exchanging contracts in early October, with a four-week deadline to vacate the property. I was excited, but Allie was worried about finding a place to live in such a short time. We spent an evening browsing Auckland properties within our budget and scheduled some viewings. Then poor Allie stayed behind to manage the motel while I travelled to Auckland to view the possibilities.

Torrential rain on viewing day prevented me from properly assessing the exteriors of any properties; in my haste, I only took a cursory look at each property's interior. I returned home more confused than when I left, but to avoid worrying Allie, I confidently assured her I'd found the perfect place. We submitted an offer, with much apprehension on my part, since I could barely remember what the house looked like, and Allie hadn't seen it at all!

Our offer was accepted, and before we knew it, moving day was upon us. A very emotional Allie and I left Stratford for Auckland, a bittersweet farewell to one chapter and the start of a new adventure. My mind raced with anxieties about the house we had purchased but I kept my worries to myself.

We arrived with heavy rain falling, just as it had during my brief look around at the open home. As we stepped inside, my heart sank. It was not at all what I thought I remembered. Inside, the house was small, dark and in disrepair, with rotting carpet and walls marred by children's graffiti. The overgrown, unkempt lawn appeared not to have been cut since the contract exchange, and dog shit littered the yard.

While Allie remained remarkably calm, I exploded in frustration, storming off to the garage to calm myself. After about twenty minutes Allie joined me, calmly remarking, 'It could be worse; we can soon get this place looking the way we want it.'

Her reassuring words helped me regain control. But my brief moment of optimism evaporated as I walked out to the removal van and saw that rain was pouring through a hole in the roof, soaking many of our belongings. Welcome back to Auckland!

We spent the next few months searching for suitable commercial premises while simultaneously renovating our less-than-ideal home. Finally, in March 2021, we found the perfect location in Rosedale for Forensic Insight: a two-storey corner unit with several offices, bathrooms with a shower, and a mid-sized warehouse. The space immediately lent itself to my vision: workstations, a presentation room and, most important, the mock crime scenes.

Over the next five weeks we dedicated all our time, with the invaluable help of Allie's brother Kev, to creating six identical mock crime scenes in the warehouse. We also set up a changing area for PPE, a pre- and post-murder scene walkthrough, a presentation room with seating for 30, forensic workstations complete with DNA charts, microscopes for hair and fibre analysis, and eight networked terminals ready for the mock AFIS system. It was incredibly rewarding to see the space come together, as we knew it was the first of its type in Australasia.

Allie began marketing Forensic Insight to schools, colleges and businesses, while I worked closely with Richard on the mock AFIS program. As close friends, our regular meetings allowed for ongoing discussions and testing. I'd already collected fingerprints from friends to populate the system for comparison against crime scene evidence.

Two weeks before our launch, Richard completed the extensive program, skilfully written in JavaScript and Python (programming languages I still don't fully grasp!). Testing proved successful, and we uploaded the data to a cloud database linked to the eight terminals in the centre. To populate our crime board and computer system with suspect mugshots, I reached out to family and friends in the UK. I was pleasantly surprised by their willingness to participate. It would have been difficult to use New Zealanders, with every chance participants would recognise someone they knew among the mock suspects.

The mock pre- and post-murder scenes were meticulously designed for realism. To ensure the blood spatter patterns matched perfectly between the two scenes we engaged a professional artist, who used realistic-looking fake blood. She first created the pre-examination scene, then used a projector to overlay an image of her work onto the post-examination scene.

Our 'deceased', whom we named Frank Enstine, was positioned in the corner of the first scene, showcasing severe head injuries from a simulated hammer attack. Brain and skull fragments were artfully incorporated into the spatter pattern. For the post-examination scene, I installed a high-powered UV light in the ceiling and used specialised fluorescent paint on the walls to mimic the effect of luminol. When the room lights were turned off and the UV light activated, the effect was strikingly similar to a real luminol application.

With bookings already secured from schools and private businesses, the time had finally come to launch Forensic Insight.

Ahead of the official opening we hosted an open night for police, University of Auckland scientific staff, ESR representatives and legal professionals, to offer them a preview of our facilities. I was delighted by the strong turnout and overwhelmingly positive feedback, even from the police. In early June 2021 we officially opened our doors, and Allie and I began delivering 'The Real CSI Experience' to year 12 and 13 students from Auckland schools and various private groups.

Our half-day workshops followed a structured and (I hoped) engaging format. I began with a presentation on how forensic science is used to solve crimes, explaining some of the various techniques for identifying and analysing clues left by suspects. Next, participants donned PPE in our changing area, enhancing the immersive experience. I guided them into the crime scene room, initially illuminating only the pre-examination scene. After a brief explanation, participants were asked to examine the scene and identify potential areas of focus for the investigation.

We then moved to the post-examination scene, showcasing the scene after a thorough investigation, including the strategic placement of stepping plates. Here, they could observe developed fingerprints (using black and white powder), DNA samples (hair and fibres), and footwear impressions. Switching off the lights and activating the UV lamp to reveal the luminol application always provoked gasps and expressions of wonder from participants.

After a group photo, each team was given a silver case containing the same forensic tools and reagents used in real crime scenes. They then proceeded to the warehouse, where six individual crime bays replicated the crime scene they had just seen. The participants set about collecting evidence, before returning upstairs to analyse their findings.

Hair and fibre samples were mounted on glass slides, examined under high-definition microscopes and compared against a range of suspect samples. Footwear impressions from the crime scene were compared against sixteen printed suspect footwear samples. Next, participants analysed a selection of suspect DNA profiles to determine which one matched the crime scene evidence.

The final, and most challenging, task involved analysing developed fingerprints and searching the database. At this stage, many participants would ask how we had got suspects' fingerprints on various items, prompting me to explain that the prints were in fact mine. Our computer system contained about 30 comparisons to maintain realism. I was one of them, but under a false name. Once participants believed they had identified the correct individual, they pressed the identification button, revealing the suspect's details and photograph. I then guided them back to the presentation room to discuss their conclusions and review the case.

The feedback from teachers and business managers was incredibly positive, with many recommending Forensic Insight to other schools and colleges. However, our momentum was abruptly halted on 17 August 2021, when New Zealand's first case of the Delta variant of Covid-19 was identified. The government imposed another lockdown, requiring everyone to stay home. It was incredibly disheartening to see our hard work put on hold by an invisible microorganism.

Faced with the prospect of a prolonged closure, we needed to find alternative income streams to keep Forensic Insight afloat. Fortunately, we soon identified an opportunity. New Zealand Post was ending its contract with the police and Immigration New Zealand for fingerprint recording services for police clearance checks worldwide. This presented the perfect chance for us to diversify our business into FI Fingerprint Services. We had only a few days to study the requirements, get to grips with the legal aspects of providing fingerprinting services for international police agencies, and gather the information we needed. Here, my existing certification as a fingerprint expert gave me a significant advantage, even though my experience had been with the dead rather than the living.

We were soon approved by the New Zealand Police and Immigration New Zealand as an official provider of fingerprinting services, and we integrated this new service into Forensic Insight. This made us unique during the lockdown as the only facility in New Zealand able to offer fingerprinting services, thanks to our dedicated recording room, readily available PPE, secure building, small team and efficient disinfection protocols between appointments. For four solid weeks, including weekends, we were fully booked with appointments from across New Zealand, accommodating people who had police permission to travel during the restrictions.

As travel restrictions eased, many businesses began to reopen and regain customers, but not us. Team-based events were off the menu for several months, severely affecting our workshop-based business model. However, one college, whose students were studying forensic science, was determined to participate, and we ran a well-received workshop for them. While this was encouraging, it was not enough. An occasional workshop wouldn't sustain the business, and our premises were too large for just fingerprinting services.

Then came another lucky break. The head of science from that same college contacted a company that provided scientific experts to schools for the Ministry of Education, enthusiastically recommending our workshop.

A few days later, Allie and I had an online meeting with Tony Jones from Field-Based STEM, a company supporting teacher professional development as part of a government initiative. We described our forensic workshops and explained how they could benefit teachers. Tony was captivated by our concept and signed up Forensic Insight on the spot. This partnership proved to be incredibly valuable for our business. Within weeks of securing the contract with Field-Based STEM, we had bought a large van to carry all our equipment, and were travelling throughout the North Island presenting our workshops to teachers and students.

The programme's success meant we were rarely using the Forensic Insight premises. With heavy hearts, we decided to close the crime centre and relocate to a smaller, more affordable space, focusing solely on fingerprinting and consulting services.

It was gutting to see two years of creative effort and significant investment in the crime centre brought to a standstill by a virus, but such is the nature of business. I still dream of opening a larger centre someday, but mentioning this to Allie now might have some serious marital consequences, starting with a quick swift kick to the nuts!

As life returned to normal post-Covid, Forensic Insight thrived, becoming increasingly popular in mainstream schools. We extended our reach to alternative education settings, working with students who, for various reasons — bullying, mental health challenges, expulsion — didn't thrive in traditional schools. I recall a visit to one such centre, where the manager warned us that many students had short attention spans and often disengaged from workshops after about 30 minutes. This presented a bit of a challenge: how the hell were we going to keep them entertained while still learning?

Upon arrival, I observed a group of thirteen- to seventeen-year olds, some already looking pretty restless. Allie and I quickly set up and got started. To our amazement, the ten students in the workshop were completely captivated for the entire day, actively participating and taking notes. The centre manager was actually moved to tears, telling us it was the first time she'd seen those particular students work together so effectively and enthusiastically. They learned without even realising they were learning. We made several return visits, modifying the crime scenes and suspects to maintain interest and engagement.

Then of course life threw us another curveball. A change of government led to a shift in educational priorities, moving back to a focus on basic numeracy and literacy. This resulted in the complete withdrawal of government funding for companies providing specialist, non-mainstream educational services like ours. While our consultancy and fingerprinting services remained unaffected, I missed the interaction with teachers and students that had formed such a crucial part of our work. Fortunately, several private schools continued to contract our services, and some of the schools we had previously worked with under the government scheme invited us back on a private payment basis.

Our lives changed forever in May 2022. In the early hours of the morning I received a call from my brother Neil. His voice was heavy, trembling under the weight of grief, as he delivered the news that his son Joseph, who was only 28 years old, had passed away. He had taken his own life. The words alone were hard enough to absorb, but what cut even deeper was learning that it was Neil who had discovered him.

The shock was paralysing, the grief immediate and consuming. No amount of experience of death in my professional life could have prepared me for this. I booked a flight back to the UK, knowing that my place was beside my brother and the rest of our family. I knew that in those dark days, what mattered most was simply being there — offering whatever comfort, strength and love I could give.

While I was there, Neil made a request that spoke volumes about the pain he was carrying. He asked me to go with him to the place where he had found Joseph. He needed me to look at the scene through my own eyes, not as a grieving uncle, but as someone who had stood in similar places before in my career. He wanted me to draw on my experience of countless tragic scenes and help him piece together what might have happened in those final moments. It was not curiosity that drove his request, but a desperate need for some peace of mind — to know that his son had not suffered needlessly.

We went to the address, and as I stood there with my brother I felt the rawness of his pain. With as much compassion as I could, I explained what I believed had occurred, grounding my words in both my professional knowledge and my love for my brother. My hope was that, even in the smallest way, I could ease his torment and bring him a measure of comfort.

In April 2024 I was thrilled to receive an email from the Honours Unit of the Cabinet Office in Wellington. I had been recommended for appointment as a Member of the New Zealand Order of Merit (MNZM) for my contributions to forensic science. (If you're in the UK, think of it as equivalent to an MBE.) I was gobsmacked! Naturally, I accepted the honour, and the appointment was confirmed by King Charles III and Governor-General Dame Cindy Kiro. I officially became an MNZM in the King's Birthday Honours List of 2024.

The award ceremony at Government House in Wellington was an unforgettable experience. Allie, Hannah and I, and our close friends Richard and Marita, were a bit overwhelmed as I was led in by representatives from the New Zealand Army and Navy. The medal was presented to me on a red cushion by the Governor-General, who later joined us at our table for a chat. She was curious about forensic science and encouraged me to write a book about my experiences, and here we are now!

As I look to the future, my journey in forensic science continues to unfold in exciting ways. Currently I am busy in my consultancy business, where I assess civil and criminal cases for defence lawyers — a role that keeps me on my toes and sometimes ruffles a few feathers among high-ranking police. Additionally, I've taken on a position with an international emergency management company. This role allows me to contribute as part of a DVI response team, sent as a qualified expert to major incidents around the globe.

Forensic science has been a significant part of my life for over 37 years, and I hope to continue in the field for many more years. Forensics are always evolving, with new and innovative discoveries and tools emerging every week. Yet the fundamental principles remain the backbone, providing a stable foundation amid the rapid advancements.

There are still nights I wake with the past pressing on my

chest, and difficult images embedded in my head. I've been fortunate to have others to lean on and talk to, and opportunities to seek help when needed. Writing this book has been part of that healing journey.

Many feel alone, navigating the shadows of trauma without support, and to those people I would say that seeking help is not a sign of weakness, it's an act of courage. While support might not erase the pain, it certainly helps you bear the weight.

Glossary of abbreviations

AFIS — Automated Fingerprint Identification System

AFR — Automatic Fingerprint Recognition System

ALS — Alternate Light Source

AM — Ante-Mortem

CIB — Criminal Investigation Branch

CID — Criminal Investigation Department

CNA — Cyanoacrylate

DNA — Deoxyribonucleic Acid

DVI — Disaster Victim Identification

ESLD — Electrostatic Lifting Device

ESR — Environmental Science and Research

LCN — Low Copy Number

PM — Post-Mortem

PPE — Personal Protective Equipment

SOCO — Scenes of Crime Officer

TAIC — Transport Accident Investigation Commission

TTVI-IMC — Thai Tsunami Victim Identification Information Management Centre

Acknowledgements

To my wife Allie: without you, this book would never have got past the first page. Your patience, understanding and quiet strength have carried me when my determination wavered. You believed in me when I doubted myself, and for that I am endlessly grateful.

To my daughter Hannah: you have been my light and my joy. Your curiosity, laughter and love have reminded me, time and again, why it's worth pushing through the difficult days.

To my mum, who weathered some of life's hardest storms yet somehow held our family together. You showed me what true resilience looks like and taught me that even in the toughest of times, love can be our anchor.

To the dedicated team at Allen & Unwin: thank you for walking beside me at every stage. Tess, for recognising the promise in my earliest notes. Rachel, your thoughtful edits gave the book its voice. Emma, your invaluable guidance and encouragement were the compass I needed from first draft to final pages.

And to the dedicated men and women in forensic science — your work is not glamorous, nor often seen, but it is vital. You face the reality that the public only glimpses through the lens of television drama. The truth is harder, grittier and more profound than any script could capture. This book is, in part, for you — to acknowledge your skill, your commitment and your quiet courage.

About the author

With a career spanning more than three decades, over 20,000 crime scenes and disaster victim identification for the New Zealand police, Thomas Coyle MNZM is one of New Zealand's foremost forensic experts. His memoir charts not just the evolution of forensic science, but the extraordinary life of a man who has made the dead speak.